KINDER CAPERS
FALL SEMESTER

Kinder Capers is a book for Kindergarten teachers containing original and traditional activities designed around thematic units. Each activity is specifically planned to help children develop essential kindergarten skills through enjoyable hands-on experiences and active engagement. Teachers, instructional assistants, and classroom volunteers can easily follow the step-by-step lesson guides for small group and/or total class activities. **THIS BOOK IS A REAL LIFE-SAVER FOR THE BEGINNING OR SEASONED KINDERGARTEN TEACHER!** It includes:

* HIGH INTEREST, DEVELOPMENTALLY APPROPRIATE, INTERDISCIPLINARY CURRICULUM
* THEME BASED PROJECTS FOR SMALL GROUP AND WHOLE CLASS TEACHING
* ORIGINAL MUSIC FOR SPECIAL OCCASIONS AND SPECIAL PEOPLE
* MULTICULTURAL PROJECTS AND MUSIC
* FULLY DEVELOPED LESSON PLANS WITH SPECIFIC EDUCATIONAL OBJECTIVES
* THINKING, LANGUAGE, AUDITORY, VISUAL, AND, FINE MOTOR PROJECTS
* ILLUSTRATIONS OF ALL PROJECTS
* APPROXIMATE TIME NEEDED TO COMPLETE EACH ACTIVITY
* LIST OF EXACT MATERIALS NEEDED FOR EACH ACTIVITY
* LITERATURE SUGGESTIONS TO ENHANCE THEMES
* EASY TO FOLLOW STEP-BY-STEP PROCEDURES
* MONTHLY CALENDAR PATTERNS WHICH COMPLEMENT THEMES

WRITTEN BY VERA REFNES AND ENID MILHOUS
ILLUSTRATED BY SANDRA THORNTON

TABLE OF CONTENTS

MEET THE AUTHORS 6

USING THE ACTIVITIES 7

ORGANIZE FOR SUCCESS 8

TRAINING VOLUNTEERS FOR SUCCESS 9

OWNERSHIP 10

SPECIAL OCCASION SONGS 11

    THAT'S WHAT FRIENDS ARE FOR! - SONG 12

    A WINDOW IN HER MOUTH - SONG 13

COLORS AND SHAPES 14

    THE COLOR SONG 15

    PRIMARY COLOR MAGIC 16

    PAINT WITH A PRIMARY COLOR PALETTE 17

    COLOR WHEEL 18

    PRIMARY COLOR PADDLES 19

    THE COLOR PADDLE STORY 20

    SHAPES - CIRCUS CLOWN 21

    SHAPES - CIRCUS WAGON 22

    SHAPES - TRAIN 23

    TRAIN ENGINES TO EAT - COOKING 24

SAFETY 25

    POLICE OFFICER 26

    STOP SIGN FOR POLICE OFFICER TO HOLD 27

    TRAFFIC SIGNAL 28

    SAFETY - 911 EMERGENCY 29

    SMOKEY THE BEAR PUPPET 30

    FIRE CHIEF HAT 31

    FIRE SAFETY - LEARN NOT TO BURN 32

    STOP, DROP, AND ROLL - FIRE SAFETY 33

COLUMBUS DAY 34

    THE QUESTION GAME - COLUMBUS SONG 35

    COLUMBUS SHIPS 36

    FINGER JELLO COLUMBUS SHIPS 37

SCARECROW 38

    ARE YOU SCARED CROWS? - SONG 39

    SCARECROW 40

PUMPKINS AND HALLOWEEN 41

    PUMPKIN DEVELOPMENT 42

    FINGER PAINTED PUMPKINS 43

    PUMPKIN FACED SANDWICH - COOKING 44

    JACK-O'-LANTERN 45

    BLOB MONSTERS 46

    GHOSTLY GRUEL 47

    FOOT GHOSTS 48

    GHOST KITE 49

    BLACK CAT 50

PILGRIMS-NATIVE AMERICANS 51

    THE QUESTION GAME - PILGRIM SONG 52

    NATIVE AMERICAN INDIAN SYMBOLS 53

    NATIVE AMERICAN INDIAN HEADBAND 54

    NATIVE AMERICAN INDIAN BLANKET STRIPS 55

    NATIVE AMERICAN INDIAN BLANKET 56

    NATIVE AMERICAN INDIAN VEST COSTUME 57

    NATIVE AMERICAN INDIAN BEADS 58

    AMERICAN INDIAN FACES - COOKING 59

    BOYS' AND GIRLS' PILGRIM COLLARS 60

    GIRL'S PILGRIM HAT 61

    BOY'S PILGRIM HAT 62

TURKEYS AND FEAST 63

    TURKEY RAP 64

    FINGER PAINTED TURKEY PRINTS 65

    STUFFED TURKEY CENTERPIECE 66

    CORNUCOPIA 67

    CORN MUFFINS - COOKING 68

    BUTTER FOR CORN MUFFIN PROJECT 69

    APPLESAUCE - COOKING 70

    TURKEY SOUP FOR 95 PEOPLE 71

CHRISTMAS 72

    THE HOLIDAY BLUES - SONG 73

    SANTA'S HEAD 74

    SANTA'S BODY 75

    SANTA'S SLEIGH - COOKING 76

    RUDOLPH THE RED NOSED REINDEER 77

    QUILLING CHRISTMAS ORNAMENT 78

    SALT DOUGH ORNAMENT 79

    POPCORN AND MACARONI CHAIN 80

    CIRCLE ORNAMENT 81

    CHRISTMAS WREATH 82

    CHRISTMAS PACKAGE PLACEMAT 83

    CHRISTMAS COUNTDOWN CHAIN 84

    GRAHAM CRACKER HOUSE 85

HANUKKAH 86

    HANUKKAH - A SPECIAL HOLIDAY 87

    THE DREIDEL GAME 88

    POTATO LATKES - COOKING 89

WINTER 90

    SHAVING CREAM DESIGNS AND PRINTS 91

    SNOWFLAKES 92

    PAIR OF MITTENS 93

    SNOW CONES - COOKING 94

SNOW CONES - COOKING 94

WHIPPED SOAP SNOWMAN 95

ESKIMO HEAD 96

ESKIMO BODY 97

ESKIMO IGLOO 98

PENGUIN 99

MARTIN LUTHER KING, JR. 100

MARTIN LUTHER KING - SONG 101

I HAVE A DREAM... 102

DINOSAURS 103

SAND DINOSAURS 104

FINGER PRINTED STEGOSAURUS 105

CHALK SHADOW 106

DINOSAUR SKELETONS 107

SWIMMING ELASMOSAURUS 108

PEANUT BUTTER DINOSAURS - COOKING 109

DIMETRODON DEVILED EGGS - COOKING 110

LITERATURE LIST 112

CALENDAR CAPERS 115

BEGINNING SHAPES 117

ADVANCED SHAPES 129

FALL LEAVES 141

ORNAMENTS 153

MITTENS 169

DINOSAURS 181

All activities have been developed with safety in mind. However, please be reminded that you will engage in the activities at your own risk.

MEET THE AUTHORS

Vera   Enid

Vera Refnes is a public school kindergarten teacher in Sacramento, California, where she has been working with kindergartners for fifteen years. She is the mother of three and the grandmother of three. She writes children's music, directs the school choir, church choir, and bell choir. She plays trombone, and sings in the River City Chorale. She has been selected as Teacher of the Year, twice! The first time she was honored by the San Juan Unified School District, and the second time by the Carmichael Chamber of Commerce.

Enid Milhous is a principal of a 750-student, K-6 school in the San Juan School District in Sacramento, California. It is a K-6 school with eight kindergarten classes and many special community outreach programs. She was a social worker for many years before entering the field of education. She taught kindergarten, was a reading specialist, and served as a mentor teacher before entering school administration.

Vera and Enid worked together for nine years. During this time they developed the activities in their books, KINDER CAPERS, and "MAKING FUN" OF KINDERGARTEN ACADEMICS. They share the philosophy that kindergarten should be a time of joy where children are active participants in the learning process. They also believe that every classroom should provide opportunities for creative expression, guided play, and activities that foster the development of social, language, visual, auditory, cognitive, gross and fine motor skills. While teaching together, their program became so popular that parents lined up two days in advance of registration to secure a place for their child. This prompted implementation of a lottery system for kindergarten spaces.

Vera and Enid have presented their ideas at kindergarten workshops throughout California. KINDER CAPERS has been very well received, and is used by teachers throughout the United States.

USING THE ACTIVITIES

<u>KINDER CAPERS</u> provides field-tested activities through which children joyfully learn. All of the projects, music, and math calendar plans have been provided with the belief that children develop essential skills through high-interest, theme-based, integrated, fun-filled experiences. The activity plans are invaluable for teachers who use instructional assistants or volunteers. The objectives are clear, the list of materials needed is provided, there are ideas to generate language and thinking skills, and the step-by-step directions insure success. The assistants/volunteers, and the teacher can feel confident knowing that students are achieving the stated educational objectives. When not working with students, assistants/volunteers can independently prepare and assemble all the materials used for future projects by using the "Materials Needed" section of the lesson plans.

The lesson plans have been developed to meet a variety of whole class and/or small group needs. The way you use the lessons will probably depend upon the number of adults available to help. If you are in an area with high adult involvement, you might enjoy Vera's and Enid's center system, which is detailed in the ORGANIZE FOR SUCCESS and TRAINING VOLUNTEERS FOR SUCCESS sections of this book, or you may wish to begin slowly, and have centers during one week per month or only one day per week. The ideas are here for you to use as is, or simplify as needed!

ORGANIZE FOR SUCCESS

APPROXIMATE TIME: 2 hours

OBJECTIVES - Teacher will:
1. organize his/her students into 4 color groups for center activities.
2. make a chart listing the names of all children in each color group and post the chart in a visible area.
3. cover 4 flat boxes with contact paper to be used for center materials and activity instructions.
4. make 4 colored, stand-up markers to direct the children's color groups to their work tables.
5. make 4 colored markers for the center boxes.

MATERIALS:
1. Half sheet of poster board in each of the following colors: white, red, yellow, blue, and green
2. Four flat boxes (soft drink flats)
3. Contact paper to cover boxes
4. Felt-tip markers in red, black, blue, and green
5. White glue
6. Yard stick and scissors

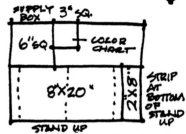

PROCEDURES: "Kinder Capers" has been developed to minimize the amount of volunteer/teacher contact needed before the volunteer begins working with children. Organizing in the following manner makes this possible:
1. Before beginning centers, divide your students into permanent groups of 6-8 children. Assign each group a color.
2. Using a half-sheet of white poster board (14" X 22"), make a color group chart by leaving a 4" space at the top and dividing the bottom section into four columns.
3. Cut 3" squares from red, yellow, blue, and green poster board. Put white glue around three sides of each 3" square and place one above each column in the 4" space at the top. Place unglued side up to form a pocket. The pocket at the top of the color group chart is used to inform the volunteer of the group she/he will be working with that day. This is accomplished by placing a card with the volunteer's name written on it into a colored chart pocket.*
4. Using the same color of felt tip pen as the color group, write each child's name in the column under the appropriate square
5. Cover 4 soft drink flat boxes with contact paper for center boxes.
6. Cut 6" squares from red, yellow, blue, and green poster board. Each of these colored squares will be placed, standing up, in the front of the 4 center boxes filled with materials and instructions.
7. Cut the remaining 4 colors of poster board into 8" X 20" rectangles. Save the 2" scrap. Make stand-up table markers by folding the rectangles in half, folding the bottom edges, and securing with the 2" X 8" scrap. (see illustration)

* The volunteer will be trained to know that if his/her name is above the red group on the chart, he/she will work with children in the red group, doing the activity in the center box with the red square in the front, at the table with the red stand-up marker on it. (see Training)

TRAINING VOLUNTEERS FOR SUCCESS

APPROXIMATE TIME: 1 hour

OBJECTIVES - Volunteers will:
1. be taught the organizational procedures of locating the color group chart, locating the corresponding color coded center box and setting the materials up at the table with the corresponding colored stand-up marker.
2. practice the organizational procedures.
3. discuss appropriate methods of dealing with children's behaviors during center activities.
4. be taught how to locate and begin preparing materials for future projects.
5. be informed of what to do if they are unable to come into class at the scheduled time.

MATERIALS:
1. Color coded group pocket chart, center boxes, and stand-up markers
2. Sample center boxes with prepared materials to use when training volunteers.
3. Copies of ACTIVITY INSTRUCTIONS to coordinate with the prepared materials.
4. Completed samples of projects. (Samples help volunteers visualize the end product. Remind volunteers that the children's end product will differ from the sample.)

VOLUNTEER TRAINING PROCEDURES - Using materials listed, instruct volunteers to follow these procedures:
1. When you first arrive, find your name in the pocket of the color group chart. You will be working with that color group. Go to the center boxes and find the box with the same color square in the front and take the box to the table where the same colored standard is placed.
2. Read the activity card in your box and set up materials.
3. When the children come to your location, you are in charge. If there are discipline problems, attempt to handle them through discussion or positive reinforcement. If this does not work, refer the child to the teacher.
4. Follow all procedures, step by step, on the card. If you have extra time, find a book in the bookshelf or pull something out of your hat. Do not dismiss your group until the teacher gives the signal. Activities are planned to take approximately the same amount of time to finish. (If you are using the system below, you will repeat the activity with another color group.)
5. Remember that cleaning up is a skill to be learned. Help the children complete this task.

NOTE TO TEACHERS - If you are new at involving volunteers in your classroom, you may wish to use the following system: Set aside two days per week for center activities and have each color group complete two activities per center day. (You will need three volunteers, in addition to yourself, for each center day.) Each volunteer starts with one color group and completes an activity. Then the color groups exchange and the volunteer repeats the same activity with a second group. You will also teach the same activity twice. Thus, four different activities will be going on in the room at one time. Before the second center day, you can simply exchange the colored squares in the center boxes to designate the new assignment. For example, on the first center day, the red and yellow groups might do cooking and an art project. On the second center day, the green and blue groups would do those activities. By the end of the week, each group will have completed four activities.

OWNERSHIP

Ownership occurs when children are permitted to experience activities in their own special ways. Every completed project should be unique and reflective of each child's developmental capacity.

SPECIAL OCCASION SONGS

THAT'S WHAT FRIENDS ARE FOR!

(First Week of School)

Vera Refnes

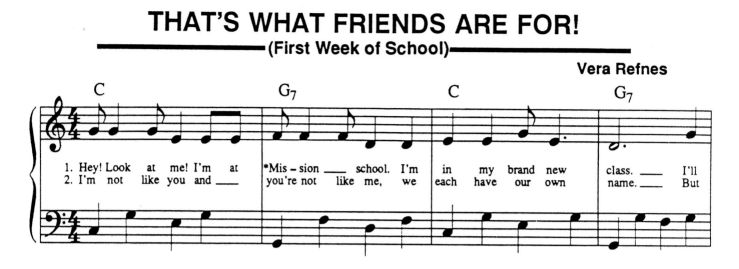

Chorus:

*Substitute your school's name!

A WINDOW IN HER MOUTH
(A Lost Tooth!)

Vera Refnes

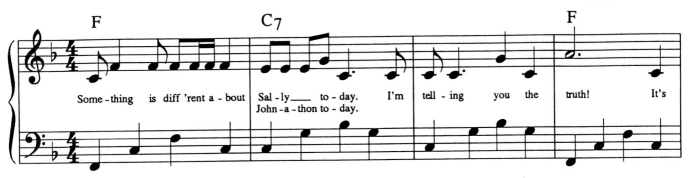

Some-thing is diff 'rent a-bout Sal-ly___ to-day. I'm tell-ing you the truth! It's
John-a-thon to-day.

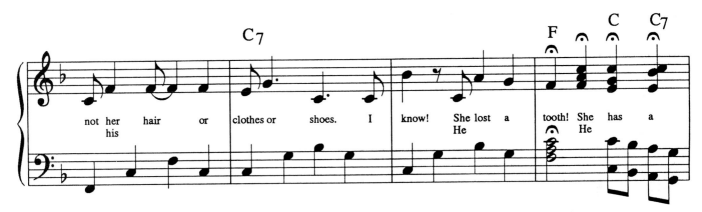

not her hair or clothes or shoes. I know! She lost a tooth! She has a
his He He

win-dow in her mouth, a win-dow in her mouth, and all she did was wig-gle, wig-gle, wig-gle! She has a
garage door* his garage door his he He

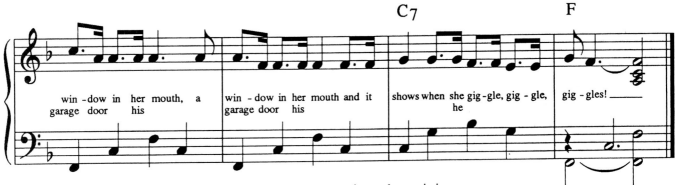

win-dow in her mouth, a win-dow in her mouth and it shows when she gig-gle, gig-gle, gig-gles!___
garage door his garage door his he

*"Garage door" can be used in place of "window" when two consecutive teeth are missing.

COLORS AND SHAPES

THE COLOR SONG
(Beginning of the Year)

Vera Refnes

Between *'s substitute words for the other verses.
2. blue - just stand up and touch your shoe!
3. yellow - just stand up and wave at a fellow!
4. green - just stand up and look real mean!
5. purple - just stand up and draw a circle!
6. orange - just stand up and peel an orange!
7. brown - just stand up and be a clown!
8. black - just stand up and pat your back!

PRIMARY COLOR MAGIC

APPROXIMATE TIME: 15 minutes

OBJECTIVES - Students will:
1. predict what colors will appear when two primary colors are mixed.
2. observe how the three primary colors can be mixed to make five more colors.
3. enjoy seeing mixed colors spread on a coffee filter to make a design.
4. name the three primary colors, and become acquainted with secondary colors.

MATERIALS:
1. Three pint jars of water with red, yellow, and blue food coloring added to make each color bright
2. Five empty pint jars
3. One large coffee filter, folded, to dip into mixed colored water so children can see the colors more clearly
4. Wizard hat, beard, or magic wand for adult to wear while performing "PRIMARY COLOR MAGIC!"

SUGGESTED LITERATURE:
 Little Blue and Little Yellow, Leo Lionni

LANGUAGE/THINKING SKILLS: If you could have only three colors in the whole world, what would they be? (children respond) Today, after we do some magic, you may want to change your mind. We've invited a special Color Magician here today to perform some magic. Let's see if he's ready! (At this time the adult can ham it up by putting on a hat or beard or by changing his/her voice to become the Color Magician. The children will love it!)

PROCEDURES:
1. Adult brings out jars on a tray, sets them on a table near the children and says, "I wonder what colors will appear if I mix a little red with a little yellow. (let children guess) Adult "magician" then says some words as he/she mixes the two colors into an empty jar. When mixed, dip a corner of the folded coffee filter into the mixed colors so children will see orange.
2. Repeat procedures in empty jars, mixing red and blue to make purple, and blue and yellow to make green. Dip filter each time.
3. Ask children how they think brown can be made. Then mix red, blue and yellow together and dip filter into mix.
4. Ask if anyone can guess how to make black. Mix all the primary and secondary colors together, and you will have black.
5. Discuss the original question, "If you could have only three colors in the world, what would they be?" (red, blue, and yellow because they could be mixed to make other colors)
6. Tell the children that the three colors, red, blue, and yellow are called primary colors, and when two are mixed together, they become secondary colors.
7. Open up the coffee filter and show the design that the Color Magician made. Display in the room as a reminder of the activity.

PAINT WITH A PRIMARY COLOR PALETTE

APPROXIMATE TIME: 25 minutes

OBJECTIVES - Students will:
1. identify and use primary colors.
2. experiment with mixing primary colors to make secondary colors.
3. create an original painting using a palette as artists do.

MATERIALS PER STUDENT:
1. Paper plate or plastic container lid (6" size) for palette - place a dab of each primary color on the plate or lid
2. Red, blue, and yellow tempera paint
3. Watercolor brush
4. Container of water for rinsing brush
5. Piece of white art paper, any size

SUGGESTED LITERATURE:
   Mouse Paint, Ellen Stoll Walsh

LANGUAGE/THINKING SKILLS: Let's review the primary colors. Who can name all three? (red, blue and yellow) What are the secondary colors? (orange, purple and green) What color do you get when you mix all three primary colors together? (brown) What color do you get when you mix all the primary and secondary colors together? (black) Today we are going to pretend we're famous artists, and use a palette just as they do. On your palette you will have the three primary colors; you are going to paint a picture by mixing the primary colors to make your own secondary colors.

PROCEDURES: BE SURE TO MODEL EACH STEP.
1. Show children how to lift some blue paint from their palette to a new place on their palette. Add a dab of yellow, mix, and you now have green. Rinse your brush.
2. Follow this procedure with each combination of red and blue and red and yellow. Make sure you lift a small amount of paint to a new area to form the new color.
3. With the palette of 7 colors, paint an original picture making sure to rinse the brush when changing colors. (Some children may end up with an all brown picture, but this, too, is a learning process.)
4. Put names on papers and set aside to dry.
5. Have children help clean up the center and the brushes. Remember that cleaning up is a skill to be learned.

COLOR WHEEL

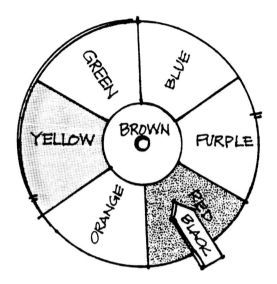

APPROXIMATE TIME: 25 minutes

OBJECTIVES - Students will:
1. distinguish primary and secondary colors.
2. practice fine motor skills by tracing over pattern lines.
3. practice cutting on curved and straight lines.
4. practice technique of coloring heavily to achieve bright colors.
5. make a color wheel.
6. play a game of finding the color with the arrow on their wheels.

MATERIALS PER STUDENT:
1. One dittoed pattern on white 9" x 12" art paper (see illustration and make a light crayon mark in each of the sections using the appropriate color)
2. One box of 8 crayons
3. One brad
4. Scissors
5. Hole punch

SUGGESTED LITERATURE:
   I Love Colors, Stan and Jan Berenstain

LANGUAGE/THINKING SKILLS: Who can name the primary colors? What happens if two primary colors such as red and yellow are mixed together? (orange) How about blue and red, (purple) or yellow and blue? (green) The new colors that are mixed are called secondary colors. Today we are going to make a color wheel (show sample) and we will use all the colors we talked about today plus black and brown. The wheel will have an arrow attached and when everyone is finished, we will use our color wheels and arrows to play a game.

PROCEDURES: BE SURE TO MODEL ALL STEPS.
1. Prior to giving the children the dittoed color wheels, make a light crayon mark in each of the sections using the appropriate colors. (See the wheel illustration for color arrangement.)
2. Using a black crayon, trace over all the ditto lines.
3. Color in each section of the wheel with the appropriate color crayon. Encourage children to press hard to make the colors bright, and to fill in each area completely.
4. Cut out the circle and the arrow. Put name on back of circle.
5. Punch a hole near the blunt end of the arrow.
6. Attach the pointer to the back side of the color wheel by pushing the brad through the center of the wheel, and spreading the brad.
7. Fold the pointer over the front edge of the wheel so that it will clear all the edges of the circle as it is moved around.
8. As you ask the children to move their arrows to certain places, have them hold their wheel in the air so you can see if they are identifying the primary and secondary colors correctly.
9. Tell children to point their arrow to the color between red and blue, have them name the color and tell them it is a secondary color. Repeat, naming both secondary and primary colors.

PRIMARY COLOR PADDLES

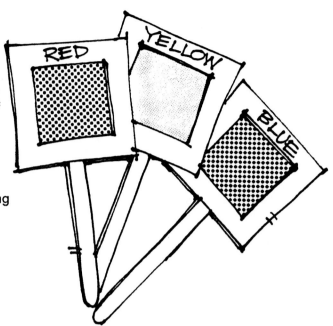

APPROXIMATE TIME: 25 minutes

OBJECTIVES - Students will:
1. make primary color paddles.
2. demonstrate independent mastery of primary colors.
3. blend primary colors to make secondary colors.
4. develop auditory skills by responding to specific words in a story.

MATERIALS PER STUDENT:
1. Several tagboard sentence strips, cut into 3" squares. You will need 6 squares per student. (Adult folds squares and cuts out centers, leaving 1/2" frame, then unfolds)
2. Cellophane squares, 2 3/4" each, in primary colors. (one red, one yellow, one blue)
3. Three popsicle sticks
4. White glue
5. One white 6" circle for adult to hold (cut out)
6. Color Paddle Story (see following page)

SUGGESTED LITERATURE:
   Planting A Rainbow, Lois Ehlert

LANGUAGE/THINKING SKILLS: What are the three primary colors? (red, yellow, blue) What color is made by mixing red and yellow, (orange) blue and yellow, (green) or red and blue? (purple) When two primary colors are mixed, the new color is called a secondary color. Today we are going to make some color paddles to hold up and look through to find primary and secondary colors.

PROCEDURES:
1. Pass out 6 tagboard frames, 3 primary color cellophane squares and 3 popsicle sticks to each child.
2. Adult applies white glue to one side of three frames.
3. Children place one color cellophane on each glued frame.
4. Adult adds more glue to edges. A popsicle stick and top frame are placed on top of the cellophaned frames. Press firmly to seal.
5. Children hold the sticks and look through each of the primary color frames, naming each color. Next they put two together to make the secondary colors, purple, orange, and green.
6. Adult holds up the 6" white circle for the children to focus upon as adult reads the Color Paddle Story. The children listen for the color words in the story and peek through their appropriate paddle at the white circle. When secondary colors are named, children must combine the appropriate colors and peek through both until they see the correct secondary color.

(The Color Paddle Story is on the following page. Be sure to pause briefly after each color is mentioned so that children have time to peek through their paddles to see the colors as they are mentioned.)

THE COLOR PADDLE STORY

Early one bright, sunny morning while Snuggly, Cuddly, Hop-a-long, and Farmer Brown were still asleep, Mother Rabbit went for a morning hop through Farmer Brown's garden. She loved to look at the round, colorful fruits and vegetables. As she hopped along, she saw a big RED apple. Right beside it there was another tree with a huge, YELLOW lemon! As she stood on her tiptoes to get a better look, she almost stepped on a BLUEberry. "Imagine that," she thought. "All of the primary colors, RED, BLUE, and YELLOW are right here together. I wonder if Farmer Brown planned it that way? Perhaps, if I hurry, I can find some secondary colors too!"

Sure enough, as she hopped through the narrow path, just above her head hung a juicy-looking PURPLE plum, and tucked in a corner of the garden, near the fence, grew a vine with a little ORANGE pumpkin. As she hurried down the path toward her home, she stopped for a moment to admire a GREEN head of lettuce. She was tempted to take a tiny nibble because this was her favorite food. However, she knew she shouldn't take something that didn't belong to her. Besides, it was time to hop home to wake up her bunny children. As she squeezed under the gate to start home, she smiled. There, in the dirt, she saw a small bunny's paw print. "Oh, no," she said. "Hop-a-long has been here too. I'll bet he came here because he wanted to see the beautiful RED, YELLOW, BLUE, PURPLE, ORANGE, AND GREEN fruits and vegetables in Farmer Brown's lovely garden! Oh well, I'm sure he is safely home again." And off she hopped to wake up Snuggly, Cuddly, and Hop-a-long.

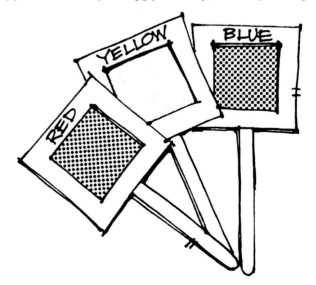

SHAPES - CIRCUS CLOWN

APPROXIMATE TIME: 25 minutes

OBJECTIVES - Students will:
1. visually distinguish circles, squares, triangles, and diamonds.
2. fold circles to make half circles.
3. discover that squares can look like diamonds if turned with the corners up and down.
4. practice fine motor skills by cutting, coloring, and pasting.
5. practice spacial concepts.

MATERIALS PER STUDENT:
1. Two contrasting colors of triangles cut from 9" squares for clown's clothing
2. Two pre-cut pink circles for hands and feet
3. Two pre-cut 1 1/4" squares, any color, for buttons
4. One pre-cut 4 1/4" pink circle for head
5. One 4" (base) triangle for hat
6. One 1" circle for hat tassel
7. Scissors and paste
8. Black and red crayons

SUGGESTED LITERATURE:
    Shapes, John J. Reiss

LANGUAGE/THINKING SKILLS: Show shapes and ask the children which shape has no corners? (circle) Which has three corners? (triangle) Which ones have four corners? (square, rectangle, and diamond) How is a rectangle different from a square? (It has two long sides and 2 shorter sides.) (Show sample and ask the children if they think we could make a funny looking clown out of different shapes.) What shapes do you see in this clown picture? Let's make our own shape clowns to take home.

PROCEDURES: BE SURE TO MODEL EACH STEP FOR THE CHILDREN.
1. Let children choose two contrasting colors of large triangles for the body. Model how to put paste on one end of the long side and overlap triangles leaving a space BETWEEN the "legs."
2. Hand out large circle for head. Model how to put paste on back of the chin and place on TOP of the overlapped triangles.
3. Pass out triangle hat, have children put paste on the BOTTOM of the triangle, and paste on TOP of face. Repeat for small tassel on TOP of hat.
4. Pass out the square buttons and show children how they become diamonds when the corners point up and down. Paste buttons on FRONT.
5. Pass out 2 circles and model how to fold in half like a taco and cut on the fold. The 4 half-circles can be pasted on the FRONT of the clothing corners to make hands and feet.
6. Model how to draw facial features with the black and red crayons, making either happy or sad clowns.
7. Tell children to write their names on the BACK of their clowns.
8. Have children help clean up the center. Remember that cleaning up is a skill to be learned.

SHAPES - CIRCUS WAGON

APPROXIMATE TIME: 25 minutes

OBJECTIVES - Students will:
1. visually discriminate and identify shapes.
2. draw a circus animal.
3. use spacing techniques to place bars on the wagon.
4. practice fine motor cutting skills.
5. practice auditory skills by following specific directions.

MATERIALS PER STUDENT:
1. One 9" X 12" white art paper
2. Two 3" pre-cut circles for wheels (any color)
3. One 3" X 12" pre-cut fancy roof for the top of the circus animal wagon.
4. Six 9" X 1/2" strips of dark construction paper
5. Glue or paste
6. Pictures of circus animals (optional)

SUGGESTED LITERATURE:
Color Zoo, Lois Ehlert

LANGUAGE/THINKING SKILLS: How many of you have been to a circus? What kinds of animals did you see at the circus? (lions, tigers, elephants, bears, dogs, etc.) Where do you think the animals stay when they are not performing? (in cages) How are they moved from one city to another? (trucks, trains, and sometimes airplanes) Today we are going to make a circus animal wagon like they used in the olden days to move animals from city to city. We will be using many of the shapes that you already know!

PROCEDURES:
1. Pass out 9" X 12" white art paper and crayons. Show animal pictures at this time, if desired.
2. Children will draw their favorite circus animal in the middle of the paper. (color darkly)
3. Pass out 6 long rectangular strips to each child, and have children space them evenly, right over the animal they drew, to give a cage effect. Paste strips on paper.
4. Next pass out 2 circles to each child. Have children paste these on the wagon with one-half of the wheel extending over the edge of the cage.
5. Pass out pre-cut fancy roof, and have children paste it on top of the cage.
6. Have children write their names on the back of the circus animal wagon.
7. Have children help clean up the center area.

SHAPES - TRAIN

APPROXIMATE TIME: 25 minutes

OBJECTIVES - Students will:
1. develop auditory skills by following step-by-step directions to draw a train.
2. visually and orally identify and name rectangle, circle, square, triangle, and oval shapes.
3. use fine motor skills to draw a train using and naming the shapes.
4. develop language skills by discussing trains and the meaning of freight.

MATERIALS PER STUDENT:
1. One 12" X 18" white art paper
2. Box of 8 crayons or access to crayons of various colors
3. Six self-stick black dots (3/4" size) or construction paper dots
4. Pictures of a rectangle. triangle, square, circle, and oval (optional)

SUGGESTED LITERATURE:
> Freight Train, Donald Crews

LANGUAGE/THINKING SKILLS: Can you think of some things trains carry besides passengers? (food, livestock, automobiles, furniture, etc.) Does anyone know what we call that kind of train? (freight train) We call all the items they carry freight. Today we are going to draw an old-fashioned freight train using many of the shapes we have already learned. (Review shapes and discuss their attributes. Show pictures of the shapes if desired. Ask children to name each shape.)

PROCEDURES: Adult should model one step at a time.
1. Pass out white paper. Have students use black crayons to draw three large rectangles near the center of the page. Connect rectangles together with lines at the base line.
2. On the left top side of the third rectangle, draw a square to simulate the engineers's cubicle. Draw a rectangle inside the square to make a window. This is the engine.
3. On the top front of the engine, draw a rectangle smoke stack with smoke coming out.
4. On the front of the engine, draw a triangle for the cow catcher.
5. Have children color in each train car with bright colors.
6. Fill the car behind the engine (the second car) with circle shapes. These could be coal, oranges, or ?
7. Fill the next car with triangle shapes. These could be boxes or ?
8. Pass out six black self stick dots to use for wheels.
9 If desired, draw the tracks.
10. Put names on the back and have children clean the center.

TRAIN ENGINES TO EAT - COOKING

APPROXIMATE TIME: 25 minutes

OBJECTIVES - Students will:
1. visually discriminate rectangles, squares, circles, and triangles, and discuss their attributes.
2. develop auditory skills by following directions for creating an edible train engine.
3. develop language by discussing various types of trains.
4. enjoy eating a nutritious snack.

MATERIALS PER STUDENT:
1. One double graham cracker
2. Two round pretzels, oyster crackers, or banana chips for wheels
3. One sesame stick candy or other edible rectangular item for the smoke stack
4. Two T. peanut butter
5. Small fruit roll triangle for cow catcher
6. Paper plate
7. Knife for spreading peanut butter
8. Pictures of a rectangle, triangle, and square

SUGGESTED LITERATURE:
> The Little Engine That Could, Watty Piper

LANGUAGE/THINKING SKILLS: If I turned my back to you, and asked you to describe a shape so that I would know what it was, do you think you could describe it without using its name? Let's try it. (Call on one person to pick up a shape and describe it, then you guess what it is. Repeat the procedure until all the shapes have been described.) Today we are going to use these shapes to make a special kind of train engine, an ENGINE TO EAT! There are many other types of train engines. Some use coal or wood to heat water to make steam which makes the wheels move. Most of our trains today use diesel fuel like many of our automobiles use. The engines we will make today will not use fuel. Instead they will give your body fuel by providing a nutritious snack to give you energy to move.

PROCEDURES:
1. Wash hands.
2. Show sample and pass out paper plates. (circles)
3. Show one double graham cracker, and ask what shape it is. (rectangle) Give one to each child with a scoop of peanut butter and a knife. (Caution the children about crackers breaking easily and tell them they can use the peanut butter to fix any breaks.)
4. Spread peanut butter, add two round pretzels for wheels, a sesame stick for the smoke stack, and a triangular piece of fruit roll for the cow catcher. (As they put these on, discuss the real purpose of a smoke stack and cow catcher, and whether a real engine would have only two wheels.)
5. Eat the engines, and see if the children are full of energy!
6. Have the children help clean the center area.

SAFETY

STOP

POLICE OFFICER

APPROXIMATE TIME: 3O minutes

OBJECTIVES - Students will:
1. use language to discuss a police officer's job.
2. visually identify and name shapes.
3. use fine motor skills to cut circles from squares.
4. find middle by folding.
5. apply auditory skills by following directions.
6. practice proper use of paste and scissors.

MATERIALS PER STUDENT:
1. One 3" x 3" blue square with pre-traced hat to cut
2. One 3" x 3" beige square - head
3. One 4 1/2" x 6" blue rectangle - body
4. One 4 1/2" x 6" blue rectangle - legs
5. One 4 1/2" x 4 1/2" blue square - arms
6. One 1 1/2" x 1 1/2" beige square - hands
7. One 1 1/2" x 1 1/2" black square - boots
8. Black and red crayons for face
9. Stars for badges on hat and body
10. Paste, scissors, and wipe rags

SUGGESTED LITERATURE:
Curious George Visits a Police Station,
Margaret Rey and Alan J. Shalleek

LANGUAGE/THINKING SKILLS: What do police officers wear? (uniforms, badges, guns, boots) Where do we see them? (in cars, on motorcycles, etc.) Does anyone know a police officer? What kind of jobs might a police officer do? (Show them the sample of the police officer they will be making.) Today we are going to make a police officer to remind us that they are our friends, and that their job is to help keep our city safe.

PROCEDURES: BE SURE TO MODEL EACH OF THE FOLLOWING STEPS.
1. Pass out a large beige square, make a circle out of it by cutting off the corners. (This helps students visually understand the differences between a circle and a square.)
2. Cut out traced hats, fold the bill and paste on FRONT of face at the TOP.
3. Using black and red crayons, draw the face on the beige circle.
4. Pass out one blue 4 1/2" X 6" rectangle, paste face on FRONT of rectangle.
5. Using the other large blue rectangle, fold lengthwise to find the middle, then open and cut along fold to make legs.
6. Using blue square, fold in half, and cut on fold to make arms.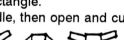
7. Paste arms and legs on BACK of rectangle body. Show how arms and legs can go in several directions.
8. Pass out small beige squares. Have the children keep one on TOP of the other for cutting. Round off 2 corners for hands. Paste on BACK of arms.
9. Using small black squares, round off two corners for boots.
10. Paste one star on the hat, and one on the body for badges. Have children write their names on the back of the police officer.
11. Have children help clean up the center.

STOP SIGN FOR POLICE OFFICER TO HOLD

APPROXIMATE TIME: 15 minutes

OBJECTIVES - Students will:
1. use visual skills to compare a stop sign with a stop signal.
2. practice cutting and tracing to develop fine motor skills.
3. spell "STOP" and learn what it means.
4. make a stop sign to go with the police officer project.

MATERIALS PER STUDENT:
1. One 4 1/2" red square with dittoed stop sign
2. Blue tag board stick 3/4" X 8"
3. White glue, paste, or roll on glue
4. Black crayons and scissors

SUGGESTED LITERATURE:
   I Read Signs, Tana Hoban

LANGUAGE/THINKING SKILLS: What do you know about the jobs of a police officer? Do the police ever direct traffic? Sometimes police use signs to tell people what to do. (Show them the sample stop sign.) Where have you seen it before? What is the difference between a stop signal and a stop sign? (The signal tells three things, the stop sign tells one thing. A stop sign is usually found where there is less traffic. One shows colors and the other spells the word STOP.) How do you know when to go when there is a stop sign instead of a signal? (Continue the discussion until they know the purpose of the sign. Have them spell the word STOP several times.)

PROCEDURES: BE SURE TO MODEL EACH OF THE FOLLOWING STEPS.
1. Pass out red dittoed sign and a black crayon. Have them trace carefully over all lines. (pressing hard)
2. Cut out stop sign
3. Pass out blue sticks and apply glue to the top of each stick.
4. Glue sign to stick and hold until dry enough.
5. Put names on back and attach to the police officer's hand.
6. Have children help clean up the center.

TRAFFIC SIGNAL

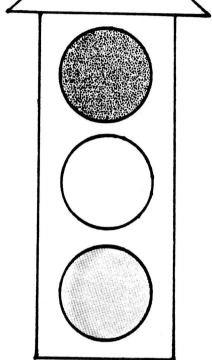

APPROXIMATE TIME: 2O minutes

OBJECTIVES - Students will:
1. develop language skills by discussing the function of a traffic signal.
2. name shapes.
3. demonstrate comprehension of the spatial terms top, middle and bottom by placing the signal colors appropriately.
4. use fine motor skills to make circles out of squares.
5. apply auditory skills by following specific directions.
6. practice proper use of paste and scissors.

MATERIALS PER STUDENT:
1. One 4 1/2" X 12" black rectangle
2. One 3" yellow square
3. One 3" red square
4. One 3" green square
5. One triangle made from folding a 5" black square
6. Paste or glue
7. Scissors

SUGGESTED LITERATURE:
Red Light, Green Light, Margaret Wise Brown

LANGUAGE/THINKING SKILLS: What is a traffic signal? Where would you see it? What color is on the TOP, the MIDDLE and the BOTTOM? What does each color mean? What is the difference between a stop sign and a traffic signal? (The signal tells three things, the stop sign tells one. A traffic signal is usually found where there is more traffic. The traffic signal has colors and the stop sign spells the word, STOP.) Today we are going to make a traffic signal out of squares, a rectangle and a triangle.

PROCEDURES: BE SURE TO MODEL STEPS #1-5.
1. Pass out materials only as needed for each step.
2. Put paste or glue on the TOP of the black rectangle and paste the triangle on the TOP of the rectangle.
3. Using scissors, round the corners of the squares to make circles.
4. Paste on colored circles. (Helpful hint - For better spacing, first paste red at the top, then green at the bottom and center yellow between the two.)
5. Write names on the back.
6. Have the children clean up the area.

SAFETY - 911 EMERGENCY

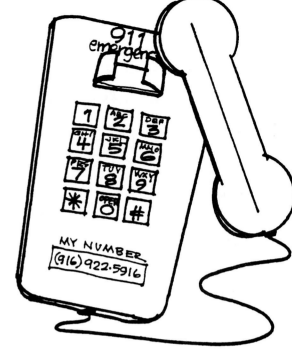

APPROXIMATE TIME: 25 minutes

OBJECTIVES - Students will:
1. state the 911 number and its purpose.
2. use language skills to discuss when it is appropriate to use the 911 number.
3. make a paper telephone to help locate the numbers, 911.
4. use language skills to dramatize dialing the number and giving pertinent information.

MATERIALS PER STUDENT:
1. Dittoed phone and receiver on 9" X 12" tagboard (see pattern illustration)
2. One 20" piece of yarn or string
3. Red crayon
4. Scotch tape
5. White glue
6. Flair pen per group of 8 children
7. Class list with children's telephone numbers listed (optional)

SUGGESTED LITERATURE:
Dinosaurs, Beware!, Marc Brown and Stephen Krensky

LANGUAGE/THINKING SKILLS: What do you think the word "emergency" means? (something that happens when help is needed) Can you think of some emergencies? (fire, a bad fall, a car accident, when an adult cannot speak to you and appears to be asleep and won't wake up, drownings, etc.) Do any of you know the emergency telephone number? (911) Would you ever really call it just to practice dialing it, or to play a joke, or to be funny? (No, you might prevent someone who is really hurt from getting help.) If you had a real emergency, you would dial 911 and say, "My name is_____ and my address is _____ . There is an emergency. Someone is hurt or there is a fire or ?" You would not hang up because the person may want to ask you more questions. Remember, if there is a fire, never use your own phone, run next door to your neighbors to use their phone. Today we are going to make our own pretend phone to practice dialing 911. After dialing, we will state a pretend problem. If you don't know your address, always stay on the line and they can find out where you live.

PROCEDURES:

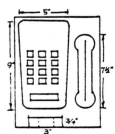

1. Child cuts out dittoed telephone and receiver.
2. Child cuts out dittoed rectangle, folds it on the dotted lines, and adult helps glue it to the phone for hanging the receiver.
3. If class list is provided, the adult writes the children's numbers on their telephones, with area code.
4. Using a red crayon, child traces around numbers 9 and 1.
5. Attach the receiver to the telephone with tape and string.
6. Have each child think of an emergency situation, and take turns dialing 911. Adult acts as the 911 operator, and asks appropriate questions.
7. Have children put names on back and clean the center.

SMOKEY THE BEAR PUPPET

APPROXIMATE TIME: 40 minutes (It may also be done in 2 sessions.)

OBJECTIVES - Students will:
1. use language skills to discuss the real Smokey the Bear for our fire safety unit.
2. practice cutting on curves to develop fine motor skills.
3. practice new crayon technique for coloring.
4. make a puppet for a drama experience.

MATERIALS PER STUDENT:
1. Dittoed Smokey Bear head on 9" X 12" white art paper
2. Dittoed Smokey Bear body on 9" X 12" white art paper
3. Dittoed Smokey Bear hat on 9" X 12" white art paper (2 per sheet)
4. Paper bag, lunch size
5. Peeled brown, red, and blue crayons
6. Scissors, and paste or glue

SUGGESTED LITERATURE:
Smokey The Bear, Jane Werner Watson,

LANGUAGE/THINKING SKILLS: Smokey the Bear was a real bear that was injured in a forest fire in California. He was burned on his face and body, and had to have special animal doctors who saved his life. He got well and lived at Folsom Zoo until he died in 1985. His mate, Alice, and his son, Ensign, still live at Folsom Zoo. Before he died, he helped remind all people to be careful to prevent forest fires. Today we see another bear wearing a Ranger Hat and a pair of dungarees. He is called Smokey the Bear. Has anyone seen this Smokey? Why do we want to prevent forest fires? Would you like to make a Smokey Bear puppet to help you remind others to be careful so that forest fires are not caused by accident?

PROCEDURES: BE SURE TO MODEL EACH STEP.
1. Pass out the body part of the puppet. Trace over the mouth part with a red crayon. Color the tongue a bright red. Using the side of the red crayon, color the rest of the mouth a lighter red.
2. Using a black crayon, outline all the rest of the puppet parts by tracing over all the ditto lines. Fill in some black circles for pads on the feet.
3. Use side of a brown crayon to color all except the eyes.
4. Color the eyes blue.
5. Cut around the outside edges of puppet parts and hat.
6. Turn the flap side of the bag towards you, and pick up the flap. Put paste under the flap and on down to the bottom of the bag. Paste the body on the bag.
7. Now put paste on the flap and paste the head to the flap.
8. Paste the hat to the top of the head.
9. Write name on back of Smokey and clean center.
10. Children will enjoy using their puppets to sing "Smokey the Bear."

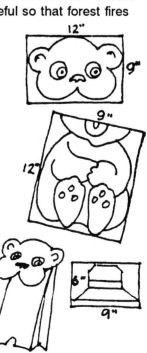

FIRE CHIEF HAT

APPROXIMATE TIME: 20 minutes

OBJECTIVES - Students will:
1. discuss the job of a fire chief.
2. practice cutting on curves.
3. make props for creative drama experiences.
4. practice auditory skills by following directions.

MATERIALS PER STUDENT:
1. One 12" X 18" red construction paper with hat pattern traced on it (see pattern illustration on back)
2. One 3" yellow square with dittoed fire chief emblem (see pattern illustration on back)
3. Paste or glue
4. Scissors
5. Black crayons

SUGGESTED LITERATURE:
    Fire Engines, Anne Rockwell

LANGUAGE/THINKING SKILLS: Fire fighters are very important community helpers. They put out fires and they also help injured or sick people who are waiting for an ambulance to take them to the hospital. What is a fire chief? (He is the boss of fire fighters) What does he do? (He helps the fire fighters plan the best way to fight a fire.) Have you ever seen him riding in a special car? Do you think he was a fireman before he became the chief? Could a woman be a fire chief? Would you like to become a fire chief? Why or why not?

PROCEDURES: BE SURE TO MODEL EACH STEP FOR THE CHILDREN.
1. Cut carefully on the traced lines to make the fire hat.
2. Trace with black crayon over the words on the yellow fire badge.
3. Cut on the lines to make the yellow badge.
4. Paste or glue the badge to the hat.
5. Write names on the under side of the hat.
6. Clean up and put on Fire Chief Hats.
7. Read Fire Engines to the group.

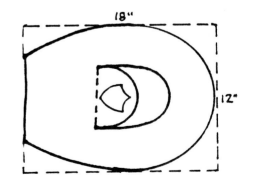

FIRE SAFETY - LEARN NOT TO BURN

APPROXIMATE TIME: 25 minutes

OBJECTIVES - Students will:
1. learn what to do if their house catches on fire.
2. practice rolling out of bed and crawling on the floor.
3. determine whether to open their "bedroom door" or crawl out of a "window."
4. prepare to locate an outside, family meeting place in case of a fire.
5. draw a picture of the family meeting place.

MATERIALS PER STUDENT:
1. Chairs or a low table to simulate a bed
2. Felt board or chalk board to simulate a bedroom door
3. Simulated window area
4. Bell or alarm to simulate a smoke alarm
5. One 12" X 18" white art paper
6. Crayons or felt-tip pens

SUGGESTED LITERATURE:
   Poinsettia And The Firefighters, Felicia Bond

LANGUAGE/THINKING SKILLS: How many of you have smoke alarms in your homes? Have you ever heard it go off? What causes it to sound the alarm? (smoke from burned toast, a fireplace, etc.) If your smoke alarm went off at night, you would have to act as if there really were a fire in the house. When something burns, the smoke goes up to the ceiling. Smoke is very bad for you to breathe so you should always crawl along the floor during a fire. Today we are going to practice what to do if you really had a fire in your house. I'll help you decide whether you should open your door or crawl out a window to get outside. Once you are outside, it is very important to meet your family in a special place so your mom and dad will know you are safe. I want you to be thinking of a meeting place near your house, and later you can draw a picture of that special place.

PROCEDURES:
1. Let's set up a pretend bedroom. These 3 chairs can be your bed, these 2 chairs can be the window, and we'll use this flannel board propped on this chair for the door. Who will be first?
2. Child lies on bed pretending to be asleep. When the bell rings, he/she rolls out of bed, crawls to the closed door, and feels it with the back of his/her hand. Adult asks, "Is it warm? If child says yes, he/she crawls to the window and crawls out. If he/she says no, he/she opens the door and crawls to the nearest door and goes outside to the family meeting place.
3. Repeat for all children in the group.
4. When exiting activity is completed, have all children go back to a table and discuss possible meeting places.
5. Pass out paper and crayons and have children draw a picture of "Our Family Meeting Place" to take home.

STOP, DROP, AND ROLL - FIRE SAFETY

APPROXIMATE TIME: 25 minutes

OBJECTIVES - Students will:
1. verbalize the importance of personal safety in case of a fire.
2. use language to repeat the three elements necessary to support fire.
3. practice the technique of "Stop, Drop, and Roll."

MATERIALS PER STUDENT:
1. Candle
2. Jar with lid
3. Matches
4. Three red felt flame shapes, about 6" high for the class

SUGGESTED LITERATURE:
   Fire! Fire!, Gail Gibbons

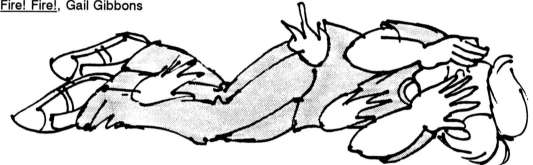

LANGUAGE/THINKING SKILLS: Today we're going to talk about something very important, fire safety! Maybe some of you have burned your finger on the stove or iron and you know how much it hurts. Some people have been burned because they didn't know the safe thing to do when their clothing caught on fire. Would you know what to do? The answer is, "Stop, Drop and Roll." We're going to use some pretend flames and practice the right thing to do if your clothing catches on fire.

PROCEDURES:
1. Stick a candle to a jar lid with melted wax and set it upright on a table. Tell the children that you are going to light the candle, and then place the jar over the candle. The flame will use up all the air in the jar and go out by itself. Have the children estimate and count how long it takes the flame to go out. Repeat.
2. Explain that fire needs three things, something to start the fire, (match) something to burn, (fuel) and air.
3. Ask where we find air. (all around us) Explain that if clothing catches on fire, the best way to keep the air off of it is to roll on the ground or wrap in a heavy blanket, coat or rug. Running adds more air to the fire, and it gets bigger! That's why the "Stop, Drop, and Roll" rule is so important. Explain that each child will have a chance to practice this procedure.
4. Have the children take turns using the felt flames on their clothes. The child's hands should be over his/her face as he/she stops, drops to the floor and rolls. The flame should come off, and the procedure can be repeated with another child. The group can say the words, "Stop, Drop, and Roll" as each child acts out the procedure.

COLUMBUS DAY

THE QUESTION GAME
(Columbus and the Pilgrims)

Vera Refnes

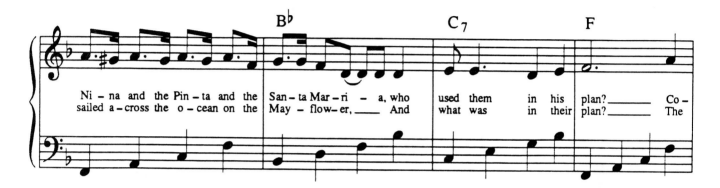

I have a lit – tle ques – tion just to ask you now__ Please an – swer if you can. __ 1. The
2. Who

Ni – na and the Pin – ta and the San – ta Mar – ri – a, who used them in his plan?____ Co –
sailed a – cross the o – cean on the May – flow – er, ____ And what was in their plan?____ The

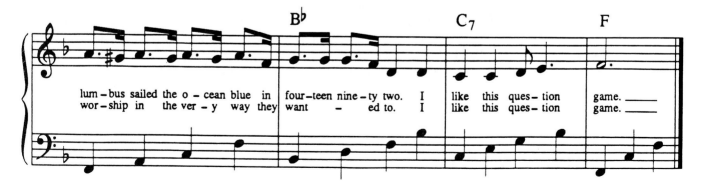

lum – bus, ___ Co – lum – bus ___ Those were his three ships' names. ___ Co –
Pil – grims, ___ The Pil – grims ___ Free – dom was their aim, ___ To

lum – bus sailed the o – cean blue in four – teen nine – ty two. I like this ques – tion game. ___
wor – ship in the ver – y way they want – ed to. I like this ques – tion game. ___

COLUMBUS SHIPS

APPROXIMATE TIME: 20 minutes

OBJECTIVES - Students will:
1. discuss the story of Columbus.
2. apply spacial and perspective concepts, (top, bottom, middle, near and far) by completing project.
3. make triangles from rectangles.
4. practice cutting and pasting activities to develop fine motor coordination.
5. locate the left and right sides of their papers.

MATERIALS PER STUDENT:
1. One 2" X 4" red rectangle for Santa Maria (the largest ship)
2. One 1 1/2" X 3" red rectangle for Pinta (the fastest)
3. One 1" X 2" red rectangle for Nina (the smallest)
4. One 1" X 1 1/2" yellow rectangle
5. One 3" X 9" white rectangle
6. One 9" X 12" blue paper
7. Scissors, and paste, or glue
8. Black crayons

SUGGESTED LITERATURE:
   In 1492, Jean Marzollo

LANGUAGE/THINKING SKILLS: (Read the story about Christopher Columbus.) Who was Christopher Columbus? (A famous sailor credited with discovering America although Indians lived there when he arrived.) When did he live? (About 500 years ago) He asked the King and Queen of Spain to pay for ships and sailors so he could prove the world was round. Before that many people thought the world was flat. They gave him three ships. The Nina was the smallest, the Santa Maria was the biggest, and the Pinta was the fastest.

PROCEDURES: BE SURE TO MODEL EACH STEP.
1. Pass out large blue paper.
2. Make waves on the bottom of the blue paper with a black crayon.
3. Pass out largest red rectangle. Cut off corners to make a boat.
   Paste this boat bottom near the BOTTOM, LEFT side of the page.
4. Pass out smallest red rectangle. Cut off corners to make a boat bottom and paste near the TOP, RIGHT CORNER. (leave room for the sail)
5. Pass out the medium-sized red rectangle, and cut off the corners. Paste in the middle of the page.
6. Pass out white rectangle, and cut off corners to make sails to match the different sized boats. Paste above boats.
7. Pass out yellow rectangles, and cut off corners to make small flags for the top of the mast.
8. Explain how the three different sized boats placed at the BOTTOM, MIDDLE AND TOP make it look like some are close and some are far away.
9. Have children put their names on the back and help you clean up the center.

FINGER JELLO COLUMBUS SHIPS

APPROXIMATE TIME: 25 minutes

OBJECTIVES - Students will:
1. observe how things can change from a solid state to a liquid, then back to a solid.
2. discuss why Columbus is honored.
3. practice making triangles from squares.

MATERIALS PER CLASS OF 32 STUDENTS:
1. Eight 8" square pans
2. One paper plate per child
3. Sixteen envelopes Knox gelatin
4. Four 6 oz. pkgs. red Jello, - boat
5. Four 6 oz. pkgs yellow Jello - sail
6. Sixteen cups boiling water
7. Two cups sugar (optional)
8. Stick pretzels for mast
9. "Pam" and misc. cooking utensils

** It is important that you have pre-made the finger Jello for the first day's groups. Each group of 8 will need one 8" pan of red and one 8" pan of yellow Jello. While shopping, be sure to pick up additional Jello and Knox gelatin for the pre-made Jello.

SUGGESTED LITERATURE:
    Christopher Columbus, Ruth Belov Gross

LANGUAGE/THINKING SKILLS: Can anyone describe Jello? Was it always a solid? What was it first before it became the Jello we eat? (show the card describing the different states) In honor of Christopher Columbus, we are going to make one of the three ships that Columbus sailed on when he came to America. We are going to start with a Jello square and make it into two triangles by cutting it on a diagonal, then we will make the Nina, Pinta, or the Santa Maria, and we will eat it.

RECIPE PER 8" SQUARE PAN: (Remember, you will be making one pan of red and one pan of yellow for each group of 8 students. These will be used for the next day's group or a snack.)   1. Dissolve two pkgs. unflavored gelatin in 1/4 C. cold water.
2. In large bowl mix one 6 oz. pkg. Jello, 2 C. hot water, and 1/4 C. sugar.
3. Add gelatin mix to large bowl and stir until dissolved.
4. Spray pans with "Pam" and pour in Jello. Chill until firm.

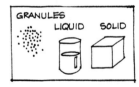

PROCEDURES: We recommend one adult per 8 students.
1. Place 2 large and 2 small bowls in the center of the table.
2. Choose different children to open the red Jello and pour into a large bowl. Do the same with the yellow Jello. (discuss granules)
3. Choose other children to open the gelatin. Adult adds hot water.
4. Using caution, adult adds hot water to Jello. Students watch it turn into a liquid as the granules dissolve. Children take turns stirring. Notice the aroma!
5. Pour into pans sprayed with "Pam" and chill until firm.
6. Using pre-made Jello, cut each 8" pan into 4 squares. Cut the squares to make 8 triangles.
7. Pass out 1 paper plate to each child and give them 1 red and 1 yellow triangle each.
8. Cut bottom point off of the red triangle to make boat and flag.
9. Arrange into a boat per illustration using a pretzel for the mast, eat and enjoy!
10. You will end up with leftover Jello after the last center day to use for special snacks.

SCARECROW

ARE YOU SCARED CROWS?

Vera Refnes

Caw! Caw! Caw! Caw!
1. Let's go look–in' for a tas – ty treat, I'm hun–gry for some
2. Let's go cir–cle low to take a look, We'll make a big loud

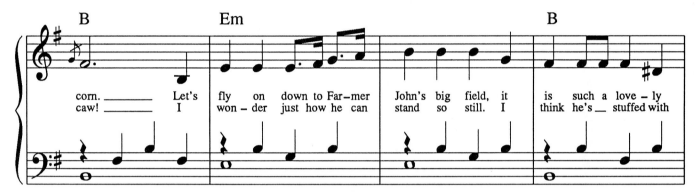

corn. _____ Let's fly on down to Far–mer John's big field, it is such a love–ly
caw! _____ I won–der just how he can stand so still. I think he's _ stuffed with

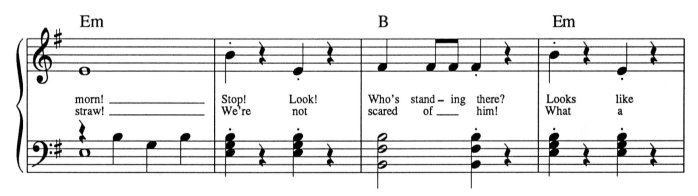

morn! _____ Stop! Look! Who's stand–ing there? Looks like
straw! _____ We're not scared of __ him! What a

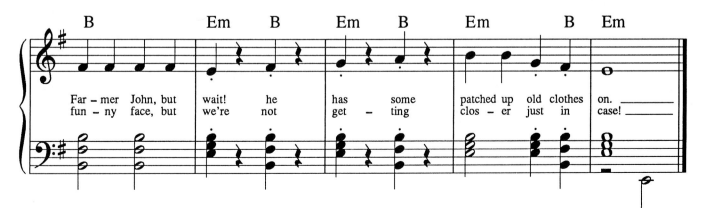

Far – mer John, but wait! he has some patched up old clothes on. _____
fun – ny face, but we're not get – ting clos – er just in case! _____

SCARECROW

APPROXIMATE TIME: 25 minutes

OBJECTIVES - Students will:
1. create a scarecrow hat with hair to wear.
2. develop fine motor skills through cutting practice.
3. apply listening skills by following directions.
4. practice counting 8 - 10 items.
5. use language skills to discuss the purpose of a scarecrow and why we see them in the fall.

MATERIALS:
1. One dittoed brown 9" X 12" hat (see pattern illustration)
2. One colored curved band for hat (see pattern illustration)
3. Scraps of colored construction paper for patches.
4. Eight 1/2" yellow construction paper strips ranging in length from 2" - 3 1/2" for bangs.
5. Ten 1/2" yellow construction paper strips ranging in length from 7" - 9" for hair.
6. Tagboard strip - 2" X 19" for headband.
7. Black crayon
8. Two brads and one rubber band
9. Glue or paste, and scissors

SUGGESTED LITERATURE:
   Six Crows, Leo Lionni

LANGUAGE/THINKING SKILLS: Have you ever seen scarecrows? What do they look like? Where have you seen them? (At the pumpkin farm, in fields, etc.) Why do farmers use scarecrows? (To scare crows and other birds away, so they won't eat the crops.) Why do you think they are found mostly in the fall season? (Because we plant crops in the spring, they grow in the summer and they are ready to pick or harvest in the fall season.) Do you think scarecrows really scare birds away? Today we're going to make a hat and straw hair to wear and become a scarecrow.

PROCEDURES: Be sure to model each step for the children.
1. Pass out dittoed hat, black crayon and scissors. Have children trace around hat and cut it out.
2. Give each child a colored strip to glue on just above the brim of the hat.
3. Have each child choose two scraps, cut patches, and glue on hat.
4. Have each child add "stitch" marks around the patches and on the hat band.
5. Each child should count out ten long yellow strips, cut diagonally on one end, and haphazardly paste five on the back of each end of the hat brim.
6. Have each child count out 8 short strips, cut diagonally on one, end and paste to the back of the hat in the middle to form the bangs.
7. Punch a hole in each end of the tagboard strip, insert brads in each hole, and attach a rubber band to one end. Staple to hat, wrap the rubber band around the other brad, place this on the child and he/she becomes a scarecrow! Use to dramatize the song, "Are You Scared Crows?"

PUMPKINS & HALLOWEEN

CAUTION: Although Halloween has been celebrated by children in the United States for many generations, it is important that you are sensitive to the beliefs of your community and knowledgeable about your school and school district policies before beginning any Halloween projects.

PUMPKIN DEVELOPMENT

APPROXIMATE TIME: 30 minutes

OBJECTIVES - Students will:
1. free draw pumpkin plant growth and development on labeled ditto.
2. express sequential order by drawing pumpkin plant growth stages.
3. apply auditory skills by following specific directions.
4. practice proper use of scissors and paste.
5. paint with watercolors.

MATERIALS PER STUDENT:
1. Ditto of pumpkin development (words only, children will draw, then paint stages of development)
2. Crayons
3. One 9" X 12" construction paper for mounting pictures (color is optional)
4. Real pumpkin seeds (optional)
5. Watercolors, brushes and water
6. Paste or glue

SUGGESTED LITERATURE:
Pumpkin, Pumpkin, Jeanne Titherington

LANGUAGE/THINKING SKILLS: How do pumpkins grow? (on vines) What is a vine? (a rope-like tube) What color are pumpkins when they are ripe? (orange) Are they always orange? (no) What are pumpkins used for? Who can describe the inside of a pumpkin? Does a pumpkin have a few seeds or a lot of seeds inside? What are pumpkin seeds used for? (Show students some seeds if available.) Let's talk about how a pumpkin grows. Look at this sample, (Show sample and describe each picture or have the children tell about the pictures.)

PROCEDURES:
1. Pass out the dittos and have children write their names on the back. Use crayons to draw the outlines of all the pictures. Do the pictures one at a time, keeping the children focused so that you can discuss each growth stage and the changes that occur. (They will be filling the centers in with watercolors after all the drawings are finished. Be sure they use the correct colors.)
2. Emphasize the correct sequential order of the pumpkin growth.
3. When the pictures have been outlined, use watercolors to fill in the centers with the appropriate colors. Set aside to dry.
4. When dry, mount on a larger piece of construction paper (green, orange or yellow paper look nice) and glue on a real pumpkin seed over seed drawing, if desired.
5. Have children help clean up the center.

*If you prefer, you may use the illustrations to make a ditto with the pictures on it rather than having the children draw their own pictures. You may wish to cut the drawings apart, and mount horizontally or make into a small book. This activity provides a good science lesson on the growth and development of a pumpkin. It is a great activity before taking a field trip to a pumpkin farm.

FINGER PAINTED PUMPKINS

APPROXIMATE TIME: 15 minutes

OBJECTIVES - Students will:
1. make placemats for Halloween.
2. participate in a tactile art experience.
3. apply auditory skills by following specific direction.

MATERIALS PER STUDENT:
1. Paint apron
2. Traced pumpkin on finger paint paper
3. Orange finger paint
4. Green paint and brush for stem
5. Tape

SUGGESTED LITERATURE:
   The Little Old Lady Who Was Not Afraid of Anything, Linda Williams

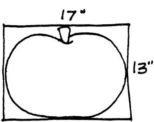

LANGUAGE/THINKING SKILLS: Pumpkins usually become ripe on the vine at about Halloween time. When they are picked, what happens to them? (They stop growing; the farmer may sell them to a store, or people cook them for pies and breads. People carve faces on them and put them in their windows, etc.) If they are carved by an adult, what kind of face might be put on the pumpkin? (accept all answers) Today we are going to make a different kind of pumpkin. We are going to finger paint one on special paper, then put it aside to dry. It will be used as a placemat on Halloween day.

PROCEDURES: EMPHASIZE THE FOLLOWING RULES BEFORE PAINTING.
RULES: Children may use fingers and palms of hands to paint their picture. While paint is on hands, only the paper should be touched! (Before dismissing children from the table to wash, show them how to stand in line with their hands up in an "I surrender" position, being careful to allow enough space between children so that no one will be touched.) Everyone must keep his/her hands in the air while waiting in line.
1. Cover tables with paper, and tape a traced pumpkin in front of each child. (Taping prevents the paper from slipping.)
2. Put on paint aprons and write names on the corner of the papers.
3. Pour a pool of finger paint about 3" in diameter in the center of the pumpkin.
4. Using fingers, spread the paint to the outside edges of the pumpkin, avoiding stem.
5. Draw a jack-o'-lantern face with finger, exposing white paper.
6. Wash hands, come back and use brush to paint on green stem.
7. Set aside to dry. They will be cut out at a later time. (If the child has painted over the lines, you may need to retrace lines.)

PUMPKIN FACED SANDWICH - COOKING

APPROXIMATE TIME: 2O minutes

OBJECTIVES - Students will:
1. develop auditory skills by following specific directions.
2. cut a circle shape from a piece of bread.
3. prepare and eat a nutritional snack.
4. work cooperatively in a group.
5. describe alfalfa sprouts.

MATERIALS PER STUDENT:
1. One slice of bread
2. Two sliced black olives for eyes
3. One sweet red pepper slice for mouth
4. One radish sliver for nose
5. Alfalfa sprouts
6. One large jar Cheez Whiz per class
7. One paper plate per student
8. Plastic knives to share

SUGGESTED LITERATURE:
  The Biggest Pumpkin Ever, Steven Kroll

LANGUAGE/THINKING SKILLS: Has anyone eaten alfalfa sprouts before? Can anyone describe their color and what they look like? (light green, thin, easily bent, like thick hair, etc.) What are sprouts used for? (eating, often put on salads) What do you do when you spread something? (smear it around) Today we are going to make a sandwich which will look like a pumpkin face; then we will eat it.

PROCEDURES: MODEL EACH STEP FOR THE CHILDREN.
1. Wash hands.
2. Pass out a paper plate, slice of bread, and knife to each child.
3. Carefully trim the crust off to make the bread a circle shape.
4. Spread Cheez Whiz on the bread.
5. Using black olives for eyes, red pepper for a mouth, alfalfa sprouts for hair, and a sliver of radish for the nose, create a pumpkin face sandwich.
6. Eat and enjoy!
7. Have children help clean up the center.

JACK-O'-LANTERN

APPROXIMATE TIME: 25 minutes

OBJECTIVES - Students will:
1. make circles out of squares
2. make triangles out of rectangles
3. practice fine motor cutting skills
4. create an original jack-o'-lantern

MATERIALS PER STUDENT:
1. One 6" orange square for pumpkin
2. One 3" X 9" black rectangle for eyes, nose and mouth
3. One 1 1/2" X 3" green rectangle for stem
4. One 9" black square for mounting jack-o'-lantern
5. Scissors
6. Paste or glue

SUGGESTED LITERATURE:
Mousekins's Golden House, Edna Miller

LANGUAGE/THINKING SKILLS: Does anyone know what a lantern is? (It is something with a light inside and is often used when camping. A glass around the flame keeps the wind from blowing out the flame. It was used to provide light in the olden days before electricity.) What is a jack-o'-lantern? (It's a hollow pumpkin with a face carved in it, so that light from the inside can shine through.) Have you ever had a jack-o'-lantern at your house? If you could make one, what kind of face would you put on yours? (happy, scary, toothless, triangle eyes etc.) Today you are going to make a paper jack-o'-lantern.

PROCEDURES: BE SURE TO EMPHASIZE THE CAPITALIZED NAMES OF SHAPES.
1. Pass out orange SQUARES, and make into CIRCLES by cutting off the corners.
2. Pass out small black RECTANGLE, and cut off corners to make TRIANGLES for the eyes.
3. Show how to make long, thin TRIANGLES or short, fat TRIANGLES or CIRCLES from the small, black RECTANGLE.
4. Model how to cut a smile. Show them how to make teeth by cutting out notches or by pasting scraps of orange on the smile.
5. If they want a mouth that says "boo," show them how to cut OVALS or CIRCLES.
6. Paste on the face parts.
7. Round the corners of the green RECTANGLE, and paste on for the stem.
8. Mount the jack-o'-lantern on the large black SQUARE, and write names on the back.
9. Have the children help clean up the center.

BLOB MONSTERS

APPROXIMATE TIME: 10 minutes for first session, 10 minutes for second session

OBJECTIVES - Students will:
1. blow through a straw to spread watery paint to form "Blob Monsters."
2. discuss the term "monsters."
3. apply auditory skills by following specific directions.
4. choose the type of face to draw on each of the "Blob Monsters."

MATERIALS PER STUDENT:
1. One 9" x 12" white art paper
2. One 6" straw for blowing faces
3. Three squeeze containers with watery orange, yellow, and black paint
4. One 12" X 14" orange or black paper for mounting "Blob Monsters"
5. Paste or glue

SUGGESTED LITERATURE:
Little Monster, Joanne and David Wylie

LANGUAGE/THINKING SKILLS: What are pretend monsters? What are blobs? (shapeless forms) What time of year do you hear people talk about scary things and monsters? (Halloween) Today and tomorrow we are going to make our very own pretend monsters called BLOB MONSTERS.

PROCEDURES: BE SURE TO MODEL EACH STEP.
1. Pass out white paper and a straw to each child.
2. Scatter a few blobs of orange paint on the paper at irregular intervals. (approximately 3-4 blobs)
3. Place the straw very close to the blobs with your chin almost on the table and gently blow through the straw to push the paint along. Chase the paint with the air to make long "hair."
4. Repeat # 2 using black paint.
5. Repeat # 2 using yellow paint.
6. Put names on papers and set the blobs aside to dry before putting on faces. (suggest overnight)
7. When dry, draw on faces using sharp black crayon or black felt-tip marker. Show different ways of making faces. (see illustration)
8. Paste or glue on larger black or orange paper if desired.

GHOSTLY GRUEL

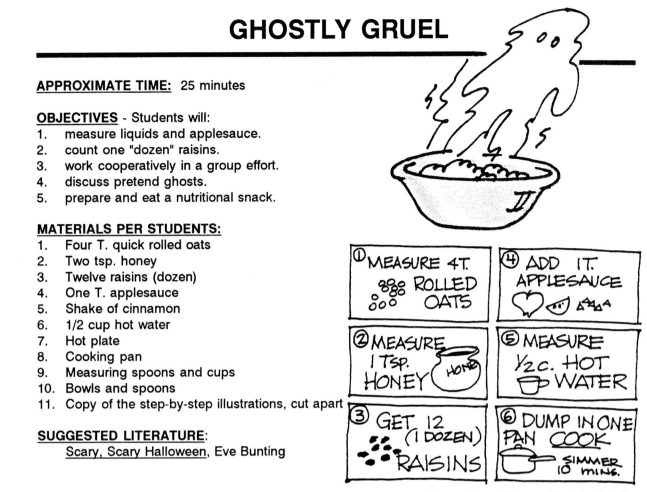

APPROXIMATE TIME: 25 minutes

OBJECTIVES - Students will:
1. measure liquids and applesauce.
2. count one "dozen" raisins.
3. work cooperatively in a group effort.
4. discuss pretend ghosts.
5. prepare and eat a nutritional snack.

MATERIALS PER STUDENTS:
1. Four T. quick rolled oats
2. Two tsp. honey
3. Twelve raisins (dozen)
4. One T. applesauce
5. Shake of cinnamon
6. 1/2 cup hot water
7. Hot plate
8. Cooking pan
9. Measuring spoons and cups
10. Bowls and spoons
11. Copy of the step-by-step illustrations, cut apart

SUGGESTED LITERATURE:
    Scary, Scary Halloween, Eve Bunting

LANGUAGE/THINKING SKILLS: (The term "gruel" may be unfamiliar to the children. Explain that it is the name used long ago for hot cereal. Talk about ghosts being pretend, invisible things that we read about in books or see on television cartoons.) Does anyone know what the word "invisible" means? What kind of things are invisible? (air) Today we are going to make some "Ghostly Gruel," and pretend that it is a ghost's favorite food.

PROCEDURES: BE SURE TO MODEL ALL THE FOLLOWING STEPS.
1. Place all the ingredients around the edge of the table so that the children can rotate to measure each ingredient into their individual bowls. Add the hot water last.
2. Place the illustrations showing the measurements next to the ingredients.
3. Pour each individual bowl into the pan and cook.
4. While the "gruel" is cooking, read Scary, Scary Halloween or another Halloween story.
5. After the gruel is cooked, divide into individual portions and eat and enjoy!
6. Have the children help clean up the center.

FOOT GHOSTS

APPROXIMATE TIME: 20 minutes

OBJECTIVES - Students will:
1. trace and cut to develop fine motor skills.
2. identify body parts. (heels and toes)
3. create a "personalized" ghost.
4. locate left and right feet.
5. compare foot ghost sizes
   and use terms such as smallest and largest to
   describe the differences.

MATERIALS PER STUDENT:
1. Pencil
2. One 6" X 9" white drawing paper
3. Black crayon
4. Scissors

SUGGESTED LITERATURE:
   Gus Was a Friendly Ghost, Jane Thayer

LANGUAGE/THINKING SKILLS: How many of you have seen ghosts in cartoons or in books? What did they look like? Would you believe me if I said you stepped on a ghost today? You did! It was a foot ghost, take off your left shoe and sock and I'll show you how to make your ghost appear!

PROCEDURES:
1. Have children take off left shoe and sock and stand near their chairs.
2. Pass out white paper and a pencil to each child.
3. Children carefully trace around their foot and toes with a pencil, then outline with a black crayon.
4. Cut out the traced and outlined foot shape, and turn it so the heel is on top. Draw on the eyes and mouth with a black crayon.
5. Have children put their shoes back on.
6. Put name on back of foot ghost and have children compare their ghost size with classmates' ghosts. (Emphasize the terms smallest and largest when comparing ghost sizes.)
7. Read Gus Was A Friendly Ghost or another favorite ghost story.

©The Education Center, Inc. • *Kinder Capers–Fall*

GHOST KITE

APPROXIMATE TIME: 25 minutes

OBJECTIVES - Students will:
1. create and cut out a ghost to develop fine motor coordination.
2. discuss ghosts as make believe and just for fun.
3. make a ghost kite to fly around the playground or hang for a Halloween decoration.
4. use letter writing skills to form the word "Boo!"

MATERIALS PER STUDENT:
1. One piece of white butcher paper about 2 ft. X 3 ft.
2. Black crayon
3. Scissors
4. Hole reinforcer
5. One 4 ft. piece of string
6. Hole punch for teacher

SUGGESTED LITERATURE:
   A Book of Ghosts, Pam Adams and Carl Jones

LANGUAGE/THINKING SKILLS: (Read A Book of Ghosts or another favorite ghost story.) How many of you have seen ghosts in cartoons or in books? What did they look like? Did they have a tail or feet? How did they move? Are ghost stories real stories or pretend? (pretend) Today we are going to make a ghost kite that will follow behind you as you walk and run on the playground.

PROCEDURES:
1. Pass out the butcher paper, and allow children to find places on the floor where they can work.
2. Using a black crayon, children will draw a LARGE ghost shaped form.
3. Color in two large black eyes, and an open mouth.
4. Write the word "Boo!" where the children can see it, and let them copy it near their ghost's mouth. If desired, they can put a circle around the word with a line that extends to the mouth.
5. Children will cut out their ghosts on the outside lines. (As the children are cutting out their ghosts, an adult will circulate and help each child punch a hole at the top of the ghost head, apply a hole reinforcer, and attach a piece of string.)
6. Have children write their names on their kites and help clean up the center.
7. Before letting the children fly their ghost kites outside, remind them about playground safety and establish a direction for running.

BLACK CAT

APPROXIMATE TIME: 40 minutes (can be done in two 20-minute periods; stop at * for first period)

OBJECTIVES - Students will:
1. make a black cat.
2. apply auditory skills by following directions.
3. cut free-form legs and ears.
4. practice paper folding techniques.
5. use paste and scissors properly.

MATERIALS PER STUDENT:
1. One 12" x 18" black paper for body
2. One 4" black square for head
3. One 1 1/2" X 4" green for eyes (folded in half)
4. One 1" X 18" orange strip for tail
5. One 1" X 18" black strip for tail
6. One 1" X 6" orange for whiskers (Teacher may want to pre-cut thin strips, as this may be hard for children to do.)
7. Small black scrap for eye lines
8. Scissors, and paste or glue

SUGGESTED LITERATURE:
   Rotten Ralph's Trick or Treat, Jack Gantos

LANGUAGE/THINKING SKILLS: Black cats are supposed to be scary Halloween animals, but we know that they are really not scary. They are beautiful animals. Does anyone have a black cat for a pet? Have you ever seen one? People used to think that if a black cat walked in front of you, you would have bad luck. We know that isn't true because black cats walk in front of people all the time, and they don't have bad luck. That's a pretend story to help make Halloween a more exciting time of the year. Today we are going to make black cats to put in our windows to welcome trick-or-treaters on Halloween night.

PROCEDURES:
1. Pass out the black squares for the head.
2. Cut off two corners, then turn the paper upside down and cut a tunnel starting at the point where one corner was cut off, and ending at the other point. This becomes the head and ears.
3. Pass out one folded green rectangle to each child. Keeping it folded, cut two ovals for the eyes and paste under the ears.
4. Using the scraps from the "tunnel", cut 2 thin black pieces for the center of the eyes. Paste on.
5. Pass out the short orange strip for the whiskers and cut thin strips. Paste the whiskers where the mouth should be.
* If you stop here, put names on cat's head and set inside.
6. Pass out the large black paper. (Tell children to put the short side next to their tummy.) Fold the top half to the bottom matching corners. Now fold in half again to make a book.
7. Take the folded "book." Hold it on the unfolded edge and cut a "tunnel" around your hand. This is the body.
8. Paste the two long strips together making a corner. Fold one piece over another until an accordion-type tail is completed. Secure end with glue. Glue head and tail to body. Clean up.

PILGRIMS - NATIVE AMERICANS

THE QUESTION GAME
(Columbus and the Pilgrims)

Vera Refnes

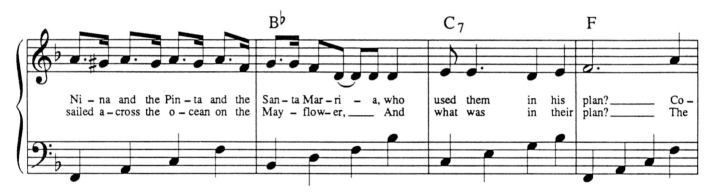

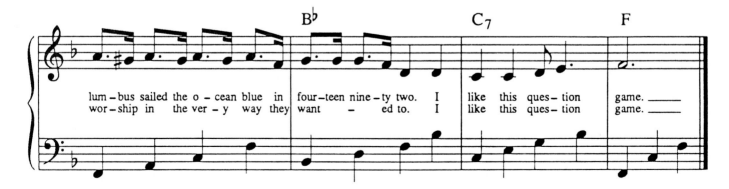

NATIVE AMERICAN INDIAN SYMBOLS

APPROXIMATE TIME: 20 MINUTES (these symbols will be used in the Native American Indian Blanket, Vest and Headband projects and should be introduced prior to beginning those projects)

Big mountain

Cross Path

OBJECTIVES - Students will:
1. choose Indian symbols to draw.
2. practice eye-hand coordination.
3. arrange Indian symbols in sequence to tell a story. (optional)
4. draw Indian symbols to develop small motor coordination.

eye

Woman (squaw)

Friendship

MATERIALS PER STUDENT:
1. Scratch paper to practice making symbols
2. Drawing paper to develop story sequence using symbols
3. One copy of Indian symbol illustrations (this page)
4. Crayons

man (Brave)

fish

friend

trees

spider

running water

sun

LANGUAGE/THINKING SKILLS: What are some of the ways that Native American Indians used to write down stories? (Someone may say they used pictures, but if they don't, you will want to suggest this answer.) Have you ever seen Indian pictures or symbols on anything? (They may have seen Indian symbols on baskets, pottery, clothing, or in books.) While studying Native American Indians, we will be using the symbols on this page to complete other projects.

campfire

bear tracks

day and night

Bow and arrow

Child

Deer

night

lightning

Teepee

rain

Day

deer tracks

NATIVE AMERICAN INDIAN HEADBAND

APPROXIMATE TIME: 25 minutes

OBJECTIVES - Students will:
1. discuss the idea of communication through symbols.
2. discuss more about Native American Indian culture.
3. practice cutting skills.
4. make a headband to go with their Indian costume.
5. practice eye-hand coordination by copying symbols from pictures.

MATERIALS PER STUDENT:
1. Tagboard strip - 2" X 19" for headband
2. One 2" X 6" colored strips for feathers, 1 each of red, green, blue, orange, yellow and purple
3. Indian symbols illustration
4. Glue or paste
5. Scissors
6. Two brads per child
7. One rubber band per child
8. Crayons or felt-tip markers

SUGGESTED LITERATURE:
    Indian Two Feet and His Horse, Margaret Friskey

LANGUAGE/THINKING SKILLS: What is an Indian brave? (male) What is an Indian squaw? (female) Explain that only the braves wore headbands and that they earned their feathers by doing brave deeds. For example, a young brave might earn his first feather for killing a deer. The deer would then be used for food, and the hide of the deer would be used for clothing, shoes, or the outside of the tepee. Why do you think the Indian Chief had so many feathers in his headdress? (He performed many brave deeds.)

PROCEDURES:
1. Show the Indian Symbols page for children to select the symbols they wish to draw on the band.
2. Pass out the long tagboard bands, and have the children draw different symbols using a different color of crayon for each symbol. (Hint - Draw the first symbol in the center of the band.)
3. Model how to cut the tops of the feathers in a point. Then make vertical cuts on the pointed end to look like feathers. Make 6.
4. Paste the feathers on the back side of the band, starting at the outside edges, and working towards the center for better spacing.
5. Insert the brads into the ends of the headband with the brad heads toward the child's head. Wrap the rubber band around both ends of the brad to make the headband adjustable.
6. Have the children put their names on the inside of the headband.
7. Have the children help clean up the center.

NATIVE AMERICAN INDIAN BLANKET STRIPS

APPROXIMATE TIME: 25 minutes (note that this activity accompanies the Native American Indian Blanket project and should be done in same day or week)

OBJECTIVES - Students will:
1. discuss methods of communicating through pictures and writing.
2. recognize a type of "communication."
3. practice eye-hand coordination.
4. create and reproduce patterns for math.
5. demonstrate understanding of the concept of top to bottom.

MATERIALS PER STUDENT:
1. Two 3" X 11" paper strips of same color
2. One 3" X 11" paper strip of a contrasting color
3. Illustrations of American Indian Symbols for children to copy (See Indian Symbols activity)
4. Scratch paper for practice
5. Crayons
6. Paper clips

SUGGESTED LITERATURE:
Boat Ride with Lillian Two Blossom, Patricia Polacco

LANGUAGE/THINKING SKILLS: Does anyone know what it means to "communicate?" Let me give you a clue. "I am going to <u>communicate</u> with you by talking." Now, can anyone guess what the word means? (to pass an idea along by talking, writing, or body language such as shaking your head to mean "no") How do people communicate today? (letters, telephone, newspapers, walkie-talkies, etc.) The Native American Indians had a special way of communicating in writing. They drew pictures or symbols to tell stories or give information. Today we are going to draw Native American Indian symbols on strips of paper, and our symbols will be in patterns.

PROCEDURES: BE SURE TO DISCUSS SYMBOLS AND DRAW SAMPLES BEFORE CHILDREN BEGIN ON THEIR PROJECTS.
1. After discussing the symbols and drawing a sample, pass out scratch paper, and have the children reproduce the symbol you drew.
2. Repeat using another symbol - they will draw as you draw.
3. Let children choose three colored strips, two of the same and one different. Put the two matching ones side by side.
4. Starting at the TOP, they will draw the same symbol on each of the matching strips.
5. Next they will draw another symbol on both strips, and continue making a pattern working from TOP TO BOTTOM.
6. The contrasting colored strip may have any symbols drawn on as long as the symbols make a repeating pattern.
7. Put names on the back of all three strips and paper clip together. These will be saved and used to complete the Native American Indian Blanket project. If the blanket has already been completed, the children may glue their strips to the blankets, being careful to place the two matching strips on the outside and spacing evenly.
8. Have children help clean up the center.

NATIVE AMERICAN INDIAN BLANKET

APPROXIMATE TIME: 25 minutes (This project accompanies the Native American Indian Symbol Blanket Strips and should be done on the same day or week.)

OBJECTIVES - Students will:
1. complete a math, symmetrical patterning activity.
2. demonstrate comprehension of the terms border, fringe, and pattern by accomplishing specific tasks.
3. practice cutting skills by learning to fringe.
4. apply listening skills by following specific directions.

MATERIALS PER STUDENT:
1. Brown paper grocery bag cut into 11" X 17" rectangle
2. 3 pre-made Indian Symbol Pattern Strips (made at accompanying Native American Indian Blanket Strips center)
3. Scissors
4. Paste or glue
5. Crayons

SUGGESTED LITERATURE:
   Totem Pole, Diane Hoyt-Goldsmith

LANGUAGE/THINKING SKILLS: How did some Native American Indians get their food and clothing? (The Indians that lived long ago had to hunt animals for food and they used the skin of the animals for clothing and tents. They also had to make their own blankets by weaving or by using animal skins.) Today you are going to make a pretend Native American Indian blanket out of pretend leather and you are going to put Indian symbol pattern strips on your blanket.

PROCEDURES:
1. Pass out one brown paper bag rectangle to each child. (11" X 17")
2. Model how to crumple up the paper into a small ball then open it up, smooth it out and repeat the process until it looks like leather. Press it open and flatten with hands. Children do same.
3. Model how to fringe by cutting into the short side of the blanket. Fringe about 3" into each side of the blanket.
4. Model how to space the three pre-made patterned strips evenly on the "leather blanket," placing the two matched strips 3" from the outer edge of the blanket. Place the contrasting strip in the middle, and glue down. Have the children place their strips on their papers. (Check them before children glue them down.)
5. The children should turn their completed blankets over and write their names on the back.
6. Have the children help clean up the center.

** These make wonderful placemats if you are having a Thanksgiving feast. They also make a colorful bulletin board display.

NATIVE AMERICAN INDIAN VEST COSTUME

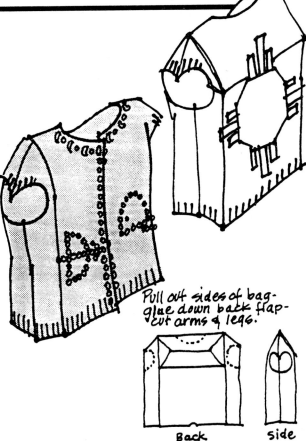

Pull out sides of bag-
glue down back flap-
cut arms & legs.

Back   side

APPROXIMATE TIME: 45 minutes or can be done in
    two sessions

OBJECTIVES - Students will:
1. make an vest for a costume or for the
    Thanksgiving feast.
2. discuss the historical way that Native Americans
    used natural resources to make clothing.
3. apply listening skills by following specific
    directions.
4. discuss cultural similarities and differences.
5. utilize fine motor skills.
6. design a repeating pattern using macaroni.

MATERIALS PER STUDENT:
1. One 9" yellow square
2. Four 9" X 3/4" yellow strips
3. Paper bag vest (see pattern illustration)
4. Four copies of illustrations of Symbols (see Native
    American Indian Symbols)
5. Dyed salad macaroni or small elbow macaroni
    (see American Indian Beads for dye recipe)
6. Liquid white glue
7. Scissors

SUGGESTED LITERATURE:
    Arrow to the Sun, Gerald Mc Dermott

LANGUAGE/THINKING SKILLS: The Native American Indians made some clothing out of deer skin.
Do we use animal skins today for clothing? (yes, leather) We are going to use a brown paper bag
and pretend that this is deer skin to make a Native American Indian vest. Native American Indians
drew pictures to represent words. On the back of our vests we are going to make the Indian picture
or symbol for the sun. What other kinds of symbols did they use to describe objects? (see Native
American Indian Symbol illustrations)

PROCEDURES: BE SURE TO MODEL EACH STEP.
1. First, make the sun for the back of the vest. Make a circle from the yellow square by rounding off
    the corners.
2. Pass out 2 long yellow strips. Fold in half and cut on the fold to make 4 shorter strips. Glue
    these on the circle at 90 degree intervals. (adult mans the glue)
3. Pass out 2 more long yellow strips. Fold in half once, then fold again. Cut on each fold making
    8 short strips. Glue these on each side of the long strips.
4. Glue the sun to the back of the vest.
5. Fringe bottom of sleeve and vest by making small cuts.
6. Using liquid glue, the ADULT makes glue dots around the neck.
7. Children will choose colored macaroni and make a pattern by placing the macaroni on the glue
    dots. When this is completed, adult makes glue dots down one side of vest opening and
    children add macaroni in a pattern. Repeat for the other side of the vest opening.
9. Using the Indian Symbols illustrations, the children will choose an Indian symbol and the ADULT
    will draw the symbol with glue dots on the front of the vest. Children add macaroni.
10. If desired, more designs can be added or children can use crayons to draw around the designs.
    To simplify the project, eliminate the glue dot symbol, and substitute with children drawing their
    own Indian symbols. Put name on vest.

NATIVE AMERICAN INDIAN BEADS

APPROXIMATE TIME: 25 minutes

OBJECTIVES - Students will:
1. create a repeating pattern for math.
2. practice fine motor coordination.
3. discuss the study of Native American Indians related to the Thanksgiving theme.
4. make part of an American Indian costume.

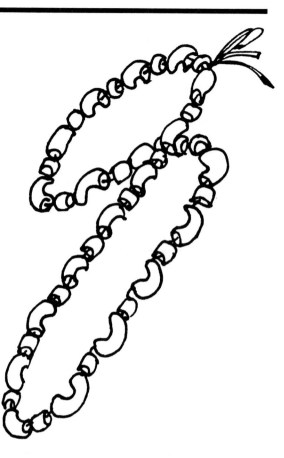

MATERIALS PER STUDENT:
1. Previously colored salad or large elbow macaroni in a variety of colors (see recipe below)
2. 30 in. piece of string per child with a piece of folded masking tape secured to one end on which to write name, and a small piece of masking tape rolled around the other end to make a pointed "needle" for threading macaroni

RECIPE FOR COLORING MACARONI: (adult activity)
2 T. rubbing alcohol mixed with liquid food coloring
1/2 lb. macaroni
Place in a large bowl and mix until the macaroni is desired color. Spread to dry.

SUGGESTED LITERATURE:
Knots on a Counting Rope, Bill Martin Jr.

LANGUAGE/THINKING SKILLS: Some Native American Indians made necklaces from beads made out of clay, dried parts of trees, animal teeth and bones, etc. These necklaces became part of their native dress. What could we use to make necklaces for our American Indian costume? (accept all answers-some may say dried vegetables or fruits, others may have made macaroni necklaces in preschool) Today we are going to make colorful necklaces to wear with our American Indian costumes at the Thanksgiving Feast or at home.

PROCEDURES: BE SURE TO STRESS THE IMPORTANCE OF MAKING A PATTERN.
1. Pass out a string to each child and have them write their name on the folded tape at the end of the string.
2. Put containers of different colors in the middle of the table, and let children take some of the colors they will be using and place them in front of their work area.
3. String the macaroni, being sure to MAKE A PATTERN. The pattern may be a simple one red, one yellow, one red, or a more complicated pattern, but, IT MUST BE A PATTERN!
4. Continue stringing the macaroni until approximately 3" from the end or until time runs out.
5. Tie the ends together and save these to wear with the American Indian Vest costume for the feast or to wear at home.
6. Have children sort the macaroni by colors, and place it back into the appropriate container.

AMERICAN INDIAN FACES - COOKING

APPROXIMATE TIME: 20 minutes

OBJECTIVES - Students will:
1. review some facts about Native American Indians
2. apply listening skills by following specific directions.
3. prepare a nutritional snack to eat and enjoy.

MATERIALS FOR INDIAN FACES PER 8 STUDENTS:
1. One 1 lb. can refried beans
2. Two slices American cheese
3. Tortilla chips (1 bag per class)
4. Sliced black olives (small can per class) for eyes and nose
5. Sliced red pepper for mouth
6. Paper plates
7. Plastic knives for spreading beans

SUGGESTED LITERATURE:
The Legend of the Indian Paintbrush, Tommie de Paola

LANGUAGE/THINKING SKILLS: When the Pilgrims first arrived in this country, there were Indians already living here. The Indians knew many things about growing foods such as corn and beans. They taught the Pilgrims important things. What did they call an Indian man? (Brave) What did they call an Indian woman? (Squaw) Why did some Indians wear headbands with feathers? (It was a sign to others that he had done some brave or important deed to earn each feather.) Today we are going to make an Indian Brave out of good things to eat. We are going to use beans to remind us of a food that the Indians ate.

PROCEDURES:
1. Pass out paper plates, and put a spoonful of refried beans in the middle. Spread into a circle.
2. Use three or four tortilla chips with the points up to make the feathers of the headband.
3. Take a thin slice of cheese, and place over bottom of tortilla chips to make the Indian headband.
4. Use the olive slices to make the eyes and cut a slice to turn sideways to make the nose.
5. Use a red pepper slice for the mouth. Eat and enjoy.
6. Have children help clean up the center.

BOYS' AND GIRLS' PILGRIM COLLARS

APPROXIMATE TIME: 15 minutes

OBJECTIVES - Students will:
1. make a collar for a Pilgrim costume.
2. discuss historical Pilgrim dress.
3. practice cutting skills.
4. compare Pilgrim dress with our styles today.

MATERIALS PER STUDENT:
1. One 12" x 18" white art paper (if rounded collar is used, pattern will need to be traced on the paper, see pattern illustration)
2. Boys - 3" X 6" black rectangle with traced bow tie pattern
3. Girls - 6" white doily for front of collar
4. Paste
5. Scissors

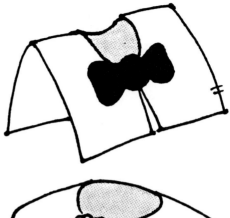

SUGGESTED LITERATURE:
    Thanksgiving Day, Gail Gibbons

LANGUAGE/THINKING SKILLS: When the Pilgrims attended church services or got dressed up, they wore white collars over their clothing. The collars could be taken off because they needed to be washed more often than the dark clothing they wore. How did the Pilgrims do their laundry? (by hand) Did they wear bright colors like we do today? (no) Do you think the clothing they wore would have been comfortable? Why or why not? Today we are going to make white collars like the Pilgrims wore.

PROCEDURES FOR ROUNDED COLLAR:
1. Pass out collars with traced pattern and carefully cut along all lines.
2. Pass out black traced bow ties to the boys and white doilies to the girls.
3. Boys cut bow tie, and paste one side to one side of the collar, leaving the other half to be pinned to fit later.
4. Girls should put paste on one side of the doily and attach it to one side of the collar, leaving the other side open to be pinned to fit when wearing.
5. Put names on the inside of the collars.

PROCEDURES FOR SQUARED COLLAR:
1. Fold 12" X 18" white art paper to make doubled 9" X 12" size.
2. Draw a "smile" starting and ending at the fold. This will be the neck hole. Cut the "smile" out.
3. Cut up the center of ONE piece to make the front opening.
4. Repeat step 3 above for boys and step 4 for girls.
5. Put names on the inside of the collars.
6. Have children help clean up the center.

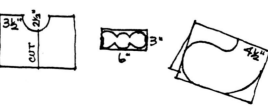

GIRL'S PILGRIM HAT

APPROXIMATE TIME: 20 minutes

OBJECTIVES - Students will:
1. make a Thanksgiving costume.
2. discuss historical Pilgrim dress.
3. apply listening skills by following specific directions.
4. practice folding and cutting skills.

MATERIALS PER STUDENT:
1. 12" x 18" white art paper with traced hat (see pattern illustration)
2. 2 each - 8" white yarn pieces
3. 2 each - white reinforcers
4. Hole punch
5. Scissors
6. Paste or glue

SUGGESTED LITERATURE:
   Sarah Morton's Day, Kate Waters

LANGUAGE/THINKING SKILLS: When the Pilgrims first came to our country, they found that life was very different from life in the old country. What might have been different for them? (There were Indians, houses had to be built, crops needed to be grown, there weren't stores to buy the things they needed, etc.) How do you think Pilgrim life was different from the life we live today? (no cars, freeways etc., very few toys, no T.V. or radio, etc.) Young Pilgrim girls wore hats as a sign of humility, and to keep their heads warm and their hair clean. Today, the girls are going to make Pilgrim hats to wear for the Thanksgiving Feast or to wear at home.

PROCEDURES: BE SURE TO MODEL EACH STEP FOR THE GIRLS.
1. Pass out white paper with traced hat pattern. Cut on SOLID lines.
2. Fold up the bottom so that the corners match, forming a brim.
3. Fold on all broken lines.
4. Bring the two side flaps together in the back, and glue or paste in place. Fold the remaining flap over the top and glue in place.
6. Punch holes near the bottom corners of the front of the hat so the strings can be threaded through the holes. Reinforce holes.
7. Tie knots in one end of the strings and thread with the knot on the inside.
8. Put name on the inside and, if desired, fold just the corner of the hat near the holes to make the edges stick out slightly.

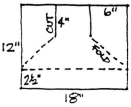

BOY'S PILGRIM HAT

APPROXIMATE TIME: 20 minutes

OBJECTIVES - Students will:
1. make a Thanksgiving costume.
2. discuss historical Pilgrim dress.
3. apply listening skills by following specific directions.
4. practice cutting skills to develop fine motor skills.

MATERIALS PER STUDENT:
1. One 9" x 12" black with traced pattern (see pattern illustration)
2. One 2 1/2" X 4 1/2" yellow for buckle
3. One 1 1/2" X 3" black for inside buckle
4. One 1 1/2" X 19" sentence strip with holes punched on both ends for hat band
5. Hole punch
6. Two brads
7. Rubberband
8. Paste or glue
9. Scissors

SUGGESTED LITERATURE:
Oh, What a Thanksgiving!, Steven Kroll

LANGUAGE/THINKING SKILLS: In 1620 the Pilgrims landed in America. They came to our country because they wanted to worship the way they chose and not the way the King wanted them to worship. They dressed differently than we do today. If you were a Pilgrim boy, how would you dress? (hat, tall boots or socks to the knee, white collar for church, buckles on shoes and hats) Today, the boys are going to make Pilgrim hats to wear at the Thanksgiving feast or at home.

PROCEDURES: MODEL ALL STEPS FOR THE BOYS.
1. Pass out black paper with traced hat pattern on it.
2. Cut out hat by following the lines.
3. Fold up the bottom flap so that the corners match, making the brim of the hat. Glue closed.
4. Paste the yellow rectangle just above the brim edge, in the center of the hat width.
5. Paste the black rectangle on top of the yellow one, to give the appearance of a buckle.
6. Staple the long headband, to the back side of the hat, just above the brim.
7. Take the long headband and insert brads into the punched out holes with the rounded side of the brad facing the head.
8. Wrap a rubberband around each brad so that the headband becomes adjustable and fits each child's head.
9. Write name on the inside of the headband.
10. Have the children help clean up the center.

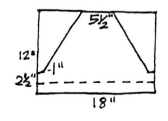

TURKEYS AND FEAST

TURKEY RAP

Vera Refnes

I'm just a tur—key and I'm tak—ing care. The weath—er's turn—ing cool and fall's in the air. I'm

hid—ing right be—hind this stack of hay 'Cause it's get—ting clos—er to Thanks—giv—ing day. Gob—ble!

Gob—ble! Gob—ble! Gob—ble! Gob—ble! Squawk! Gob—ble! Gob—ble! Gob—ble! Gob—ble! Gob—ble! Squawk! Now

I'm not a chick—en for good—ness sake! But they won't put me in the o—ven to bake. Cause

I'm so smart, do you a—gree?___ I'll stay right here un—til I'm free! ___ Gob—ble!

Gob—ble! Gob—ble! Gob—ble! Gob—ble! Squawk! Gob—ble! Gob—ble! Gob—ble! Gob—ble! Gob—ble! Squawk! Here

comes the far—mer, Oh no! Oh dear! ___ I think I'll shout, "I'll be fat—ter next year!" The
(Loud!. . . . .)

far—mer will stop, and nod his head And I'll be here ___ a—live and well fed! Gob—ble!

Gob—ble! Gob—ble! Gob—ble! Gob—ble! Squawk! Gob—ble! Gob—ble! Gob—ble! Gob—ble! Gob—ble! Squawk!

(Repeat Gobble Gobbles until it fades away)

Tambourine rhythm can be used throughout:

etc...

Tap   Tap   Shake _____   Tap   Tap   Shake _____

FINGER PAINTED TURKEY PRINTS

APPROXIMATE TIME: 25 minutes

OBJECTIVES - Students will:
1. practice a new art technique, making prints.
2. make a placemat for the Thanksgiving Feast and to be used as a room decoration during Thanksgiving unit.
3. apply their listening skills by following specific directions.

MATERIALS PER STUDENT:
1. Two 12" x 18" white art paper
2. Pre-cut turkey body (see pattern illustrations)
3. Pre-cut turkey tail (see pattern illustrations)
4. Liquid finger paint in orange, yellow, red and brown
5. Paint aprons
6. Soap and water for clean up
7. Tables covered with paper
8. Pictures of turkeys (optional)
9. Paper hole punch

SUGGESTED LITERATURE:
Sometimes It's Turkey - Sometimes It's Feathers, Lorna Balian

LANGUAGE/THINKING SKILLS: Why do we think of turkeys as the main food at a Thanksgiving dinner? (It's a tradition and it is believed that when the first Thanksgiving took place, they ate wild turkeys.) What does a turkey look like? (after they offer descriptions, show the turkey picture and discuss) Do turkeys fly? (just barely and for very short distances) Today we are going to learn a new art technique called prints, and we are going to make decorative turkeys for placemats for a Thanksgiving feast or to decorate the room for Thanksgiving.

PROCEDURES: BE SURE TO MODEL STEPS # 1 - 7.
1. Put on paint aprons and discuss the rules for finger painting.
2. Cover the tables with white butcher paper. Tape a piece of fingerpaint paper in front of each child.
3. Pour a 3" pool of finger paint in the center of the rectangle.
4. Be sure to make 2 brown, 2 yellow, 2 orange, and 2 red areas per 8 children.
5. Let children work with paint for about 5 minutes, pushing the paint to fill the rectangle. Then using three fingers, make many short strokes to look like feathers. Wash hands before the next step.
6. Pass out turkey bodies, put names on one side. Go to brown paint.
7. Next, place the turkey body on the brown paint, with the name looking at you. Press gently straight down, pick up and presto - turkey feathers! Set aside to dry.
8. Give each child the turkey feathers section. He/she will press it first in the yellow paint, second in the orange, and third in the red, each time forming feathers in the paint with their fingers. Set aside to dry, and wash hands.
9. Glue the body and feathers together, and paper punch an eye hole.

STUFFED TURKEY CENTERPIECE

APPROXIMATE TIME: 20 minutes first day
20 minutes second day

OBJECTIVES - Students will:
1. discuss historical Thanksgiving.
2. apply listening skills by following specific directions.
3. practice cutting on curved and straight lines.

MATERIALS PER STUDENT:
1. Brown lunch bag
2. One dittoed brown head and wing on 9" X 12", (see pattern illustration) paper clip to another piece of brown 9" X 12" brown for cutting double
3. Two yellow 2 1/2" squares for eyes
4. Two orange 1 1/2" squares for center of eyes
5. Two red 6" X 1" for wattles
6. One 2 1/2" orange square for beak
7. Eight 6" X 2" varied colored strips for tail feathers
8. One rubberband
9. Newspaper for stuffing
10. Scissors, and paste or glue

SUGGESTED LITERATURE:
Mousekin's Thanksgiving, Edna Miller

LANGUAGE/THINKING SKILLS: Let's talk turkey! What do we know about turkeys? (They walk on two legs, we eat them, they have a beak and feathers, and the red thing under their chin is called a wattle.) We are going to make a stuffed turkey to decorate our feast tables.

PROCEDURES FOR PART I: BE SURE TO MODEL EACH STEP FOR THE CHILDREN.
1. Pass out eight varied colored turkey feathers. (6" X 2" strips) Cut points on both ends. Next, make vertical cuts on the points.
2. Arrange feathers in a fan, and staple at the bottom to secure.
3. Pass out doubled turkey head and wings and cut out doubled.
4. Fold one circle in half (like a taco) and cut along fold. (wings)
5. Using scissors, make small cuts into the curved side of the wings.
6. Pass out 2 yellow and 2 orange squares each. Make these squares into circles by rounding off corners.
7. Put all parts into an envelope, or paper clip them together to save. Put name on it.

PROCEDURES FOR PART II: BE SURE TO MODEL EACH STEP
1. Take head and fold on broken line. Paste two heads together leaving folded ends unpasted. Paste on eyes, yellow first. Using orange squares, round corners for center of eyes.
2. Make orange beak by folding the square to make a triangle. With the folded side as the top of the beak, paste the corners to front of the head.
3. Place 2 red strips together for the wattle. Round off bottom corners. Paste red wattles on each side of the head, matching at the bottom.
4. Take brown bag, keep flat and paste the folded-out tabs of the head to the bag bottom. Paste half circle wings on each side.
5. Stuff bag with newspaper snowballs, gather with rubberband, staple tailfeather fan to the gathered end.
6. Write name on full circle and paste to the bottom of the turkey.

CORNUCOPIA

APPROXIMATE TIME: 35 minutes

OBJECTIVES - Students will:
1. make a cornucopia placemat.
2. use wet chalk art technique to draw fruits and vegetables.
3. be exposed to new vocabulary such as cornucopia, horn of plenty, bounty, crops, etc.

MATERIALS PER STUDENT:
1. One pre-traced cornucopia on 18" X 24" manilla paper
2. Colored chalk in a variety of colors
3. A small amount of water (margarine lids work well to put the water in)
4. Pictures of fruits and vegetables (Peabody kits have great pictures)
5. Scissors
6. Black crayons
7. Hairspray or workable fixative to spray completed Cornucopia to keep from smearing

SUGGESTED LITERATURE:
It's Thanksgiving, Jack Prelutsky

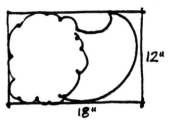

LANGUAGE/THINKING SKILLS: At Thanksgiving time, many people try to think about what they have for which to be thankful. In our country, we are fortunate to be able to grow many different kinds of crops such as grains, fruits and vegetables. We call this "rich bounty," and we are thankful for this. Can you name some of the fruits and vegetables grown in our country? (Name some things such as oranges, cranberries, corn, peas etc.) Today we are going to make something called a cornucopia. A real cornucopia, or horn of plenty, is often a basket filled with fresh fruits and vegetables. Let's look at these pictures of fruits and vegetables to get some ideas about which ones we may want in our cornucopias.

PROCEDURES: Model all steps.
1. Pass out pre-traced cornucopias, the water in lids, the colored chalk and the black crayons.
2. Using a black crayon, children will draw over the traced lines of the cornucopia.
3. Still using a black crayon, children will draw the outline of a variety of nuts, fruits and vegetables coming out of the basket. Tell them to draw the items quite large to fill in the entire area.
4. Using dipped brown chalk, make a basket weave design on the basket area. (Chalk may need to be dipped in water often.)
5. Using colored chalk, dip in water often and color in the outlined fruits and vegetables.
6. Cut out completed cornucopia.
7. When dry, it may need to be sprayed with hairspray or a workable fixative to keep the colors from smearing. (Do not use spray around the students.)
8. Have children help clean up the center before washing their hands.

CORN MUFFINS - COOKING

APPROXIMATE TIME: 20 minutes
   *This makes an excellent companion project with making butter. (See butter activity.) Both can be done simultaneously.

OBJECTIVES - Students will:
1. discuss the historical First Thanksgiving.
2. recognize the importance of corn to the Pilgrims and Indians.
3. repeat vocabulary words such as grind, corn meal, ingredients, etc.
4. prepare food for a Thanksgiving feast or for a classroom snack.

MATERIALS PER GROUP OF 8:
1. One box (8.5 oz.) corn muffin mix
2. One egg
3. 1/3 C. milk
4. Miscellaneous cooking equipment including: mixing bowl, measuring cup, mixing spoon, rubber spatula, muffin pan for 8, cupcake papers
5. Oven

SUGGESTED LITERATURE:
   Corn Is Maize, Aliki

LANGUAGE/THINKING SKILLS: What is corn, and how does it grow? (It's a vegetable and it grows on a cob which grows on a stalk.) Describe what corn looks like. Is all corn yellow? (No, some is white) What do you think happens to corn when it is dried? (It gets hard.) When the Pilgrims first arrived in this country, they were introduced to corn by the Indians. The Indians used to dry corn, then grind it by pushing it against a rock with another rock. They used the ground corn to prepare many foods. Today we are going to use ground corn, called corn meal, to make corn muffins.

PROCEDURES:
1. Wash hands
2. Prepare corn muffin mix according to package directions. Since this is a group project, have children take turns doing the following:
   a. Dump mix into bowl
   b. Crack egg into the measuring cup
   c. Add egg to mixing bowl
   d. Measure milk
   e. Add milk to mixing bowl
   f. Stir - give each child a stir or two
   g. Have children take turns placing the cupcake wrappers into the muffin pans and spooning the mixture into the cupcake wrappers.
   h. Bake according to package directions
   i. Eat and enjoy with butter and/or honey or put in the freezer, and save until the Thanksgiving feast.
   j. Have children help clean up the center.

BUTTER FOR CORN MUFFIN PROJECT

APPROXIMATE TIME: 25 minutes

OBJECTIVES - Students will:
1. observe liquid changing to a solid.
2. discuss how butter is made.
3. compare past and present ways of obtaining butter.
4. prepare something good to eat and enjoy from the dairy food group.

MATERIALS FOR BUTTER:
1. One half-pint of whipping cream per 8 children
2. See-through jar, 1 quart size
3. Salt
4. 1/4 C honey per 1/2 pt. whipping cream (optional item to use if you wish to make honey butter to eat on the muffins)

SUGGESTED LITERATURE:
   From Grass to Butter, Ali Mitgutsch

LANGUAGE/THINKING SKILLS: Introduce the terms liquid and solid, and discuss the difference between the two. Ask if they can think of something that starts as a liquid and ends up as a solid. (ice cubes, Jello, ice cream) Tell the children that they are going to make butter from cream. Discuss that we get cream from the milk that we get from cows. Explain that it takes a long time to make butter by shaking cream in a jar. They will be taking turns shaking the jar. (If you are also making corn muffins, both activities may be done at the same time.)

PROCEDURES FOR MAKING BUTTER:
1. Empty 1/2 pt. of whipping cream into a chilled jar. Explain that because cream comes from a cow, it is a dairy product.
2. Take turns shaking the jar being careful not to bump the table with the jar. Be patient!
3. Curds will begin to form, then a clump of butter will form. Pour off the liquid, called whey. When all is clumped, put into a plastic container and press with the back of a wooden spoon to remove the rest of the whey.
4. Add a dash of salt and mix. Chill, and it's ready to eat!
5. If desired, mix the finished butter with 1/4 C. honey.
6. Have the children help clean the center.

APPLESAUCE - COOKING

APPROXIMATE TIME: 25 minutes using pre-cooked apples for first day's group

OBJECTIVES - Students will:
1. prepare applesauce from scratch for Thanksgiving feast or classroom snack.
2. practice using knives safely.
3. discuss the historical theme of the Pilgrims and Indians.

MATERIALS PER STUDENT:
1. One fresh apple per child
2. One cooked apple per child in first day's group
3. One knife per child (pumpkin cutters work well for this)
4. Paper plates for cutting areas
5. Water
6. Sugar
7. Cinnamon
8. Measuring cups
8. Crock pot
9. Large sieve and wooden press
10. Rubber spatula
11. Sharp knife FOR ADULT USE ONLY

SUGGESTED LITERATURE:
   Rain Makes Applesauce, Julian Scheer

LANGUAGE/THINKING SKILLS: From what is applesauce made? What color apples are used to make applesauce? (any color) Where do apples grow? (on trees) What happens to apples when they are cooked? (they become soft) How do they get the seeds and skin out of the cooked apples when making applesauce? (they strain them out) Today we are going to make applesauce from the apples that have already been cooked, and we are going to prepare apples and put them in the crock pot to cook for another batch of applesauce.

PROCEDURES:
1. Wash hands and apples.
2. Adult cuts apples in half, and places flat side down on paper plate. Adult shows correct way to position fingers and use knife.
3. Child slices apple in large chunks, including core, seeds and skin.
4. Place all apple parts in crock pot.
5. Add 1/2 cup water and 1/2 cup sugar.
6. Let each child put in a small shake of cinnamon.
7. Plug in and cook until soft, letting the aroma fill the room.
8. Put the sieve in a large bowl and place the previously cooked apples in the sieve. (If 2 groups are cooking today, divide the cooked apples into 2 portions before placing them in the sieve.)
9. Let each child take a turn using the wooden press to squish the good apple parts out through the holes and into the bowl.
10. Scrape occasionally while pointing out how the inedible matter stays in the sieve.
11. Refrigerate applesauce, eat while warm for classroom snack, or freeze and serve at a Thanksgiving feast.
12. Have children help clean up the center.

TURKEY SOUP FOR 95 PEOPLE

APPROXIMATE TIME: 30 minutes

OBJECTIVES - Students will:
1. prepare the main entree for a Thanksgiving feast.
2. practice the proper use of sharp knives and potato peelers.
3. develop self-esteem as they contribute to a group project that will later feed others at the feast.
4. see what ingredients can be used to make a delicious soup.

MATERIALS FOR 6 GROUPS OF 5 STUDENTS:
1. A variety of vegetables and grains
2. Paring knives and potato peelers for each group
3. Paper plates for cutting vegetables
4. Twelve Baggies of diced chicken or turkey - use 6, reserve 6 (about 12 whole chicken breasts)
5. 18 quarts chicken broth, use 12 reserve 6 (purchased in cans or saved from boiling chicken)
6. Six 5 qt. crock pots
7. Salt and pepper
8. Large stirring spoons

(Note: A successful way of obtaining the necessary ingredients is to ask each child to bring one contribution from home a day or two before cooking. A suggested list might include: potato, carrot, onion, celery, zucchini, Baggie of rice, barley or noodles or any other creative soup ingredients. The contributions are divided into 6 tubs to be used with 6 groups.) The materials can be graphed for a math activity.

SUGGESTED LITERATURE:
Stone Soup, Marcia Brown

LANGUAGE/THINKING SKILLS: The First Thanksgiving celebration with the Pilgrims and the Indians was a time of sharing and giving thanks for food and friends in the new land. Each of you brought something to put in our soup so that we may all share and relive that First Thanksgiving. Today we are going to prepare turkey soup for our feast.

PROCEDURES: BE SURE TO MODEL SAFELY USING KNIVES AND PEELERS.
1. Adult - cover tables with paper, pass out paper plates, knives and peelers, placing crock pot and empty bowl in center of table while children are washing their hands.
2. Children should peel and chop vegetables, and put in bowl.
3. Adult washes all vegetables after chopping
4. Children should add broth, vegetables, chicken, grains, etc. to crock pot. Plug in crock pot so children can smell the aroma.
5. Have the children help clean the center.

RECIPE: (VERY FLEXIBLE) For 5 quart crock pot

2 quarts chicken broth	6 celery stalks
1 whole cooked, diced chicken breast	1 onion
1 cup grains or noodles	6 carrots

This makes a thick soup. To stretch to 12 crock pots, ask each adult to take home a crock pot, add 1 quart broth, 1 baggie of chicken, then divide to make 2 pots.

CHRISTMAS

CAUTION: Although Christmas and Hanukkah are celebrated throughout the world, it is important that you are sensitive to the beliefs of your community and knowledgeable about your school and school district policies before beginning any Christmas or Hanukkah projects.

THE HOLIDAY BLUES

Vera Refnes

1st verse slow
2nd verse faster

I've got the Hol–i–day Blues! I've got the Hol–i–day Blues, and I don't know__ what to do. _____ I
I've got some Hol–i–day news! I've got some Hol–i–day news, and I know what I'm gon–na do. _____ I

want–ed to buy__ a ver–y spe–cial gift and__ give it right to you! _____ But I
have__ a ver – y__ spe–cial gift and I'll give it right to you! _____ I'll__

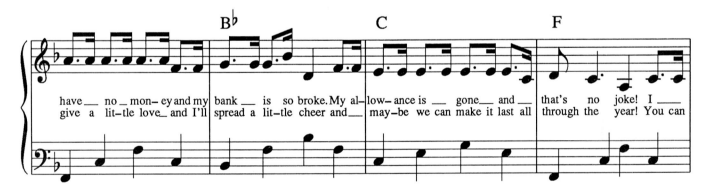

have__ no__ mon–ey and my bank__ is so broke. My al–low–ance is__ gone__ and that's no joke! I__
give a lit–tle love__ and I'll spread a lit–tle cheer and__ may–be we can make it last all through the year! You can

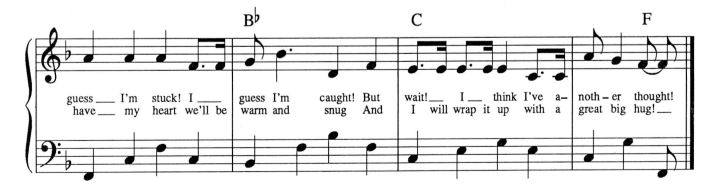

guess__ I'm stuck! I__ guess I'm caught! But wait!__ I__ think I've a–noth–er thought!
have__ my heart we'll be warm and snug And I will wrap it up with a great big hug!__

SANTA'S HEAD

APPROXIMATE TIME: 25 minutes
(Body can be made at another center.)

OBJECTIVES - Students will:
1. make the head of Santa.
2. apply listening skills by following specific directions.
3. make circles out of squares.
4. fold circles in half.
5. practice cutting skills.
6. practice proper use of paste.

MATERIALS PER STUDENT:
1. One 6" pink square for face
2. Two 2" blue squares for eyes
3. One 8" red square with dittoed hat (see pattern illustration)
4. One 1 1/2" X 7" white rectangle for fur on hat
5. One 3/4" X 4" white rectangle for eyebrows
6. One 2" red square for nose
7. White cotton or polyester batting for hat pompon and beard
8. Scissors, and paste or glue

SUGGESTED LITERATURE:
Santa's Hat, Claire Schumacher

LANGUAGE/THINKING SKILLS: Have you seen any Santas in the shopping malls this year? (responses) How could you tell it was Santa? (white beard, red suit, fat, etc.) What did you do when you saw him? (waved at him, sat on lap, told what I wanted for Christmas) Today we are going to make our own Santas to decorate our classroom and for you to take home before the holiday. In this center we are going to make the head. You will make the body and put him together in another center. This is what the head looks like. (Show sample and discuss the fur on the hat and the pompon on the hat.)

PROCEDURES:
1. Cut out hat, being careful to stay on the lines.
2. Pass out white rectangle for fur on hat. Make it look "furry" by cutting in and out. Paste it on the bottom of the hat.
3. Using the pink square, cut the corners off to make a circle face.
4. Put paste on the top of the head or the "forehead" area and paste hat to the head.
5. Make eyes by putting 2 blue squares on top of one another and rounding off the corners to make circles. Paste below hat.
6. For eyebrows, fold small rectangle in half and fringe while folded. Open and cut on fold. Paste at top of eyes.
7. For nose, cut circle from red square by rounding corners.
8. For beard, spread a generous amount of paste on chin and sideburns. Give children some polyester batting and have them stretch it out to cover pasted area.
9. Be sure children put their names on the back of the head. If the body is completed, attach the head to the body by putting paste on the back of the chin. Save to decorate classroom. If the body has not been made, set Santa's head aside to dry. They will be making the body at another center.

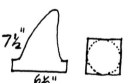

7½" 6½"

SANTA'S BODY

APPROXIMATE TIME: 25 minutes

OBJECTIVES - Students will:
1. fold circles in half, and cut on the fold.
2. practice using a new scissors technique to make things appear "furry."
3. use scissors to cut on pre-traced lines.

MATERIALS PER STUDENT:
1. Three dittoed red 8" circles for arms, legs and body
2. One black 8" X 1 1/2" for belt
3. One white 8" X 1 1/2" rectangle for fur on belt
4. One white 2 1/2" square for belt buckle
5. One black 2" square for belt buckle
6. Two white 2 1/2" squares for buttons
7. Four white 4" X 1" rectangles for fur over mittens and boots
8. One black 9" X 5" rectangle, folded for traced boots (see illustration)
9. One black 7" X 4" rectangle, folded for traced mittens (see illustration)
10. Scissors and paste or glue

SUGGESTED LITERATURE:

My Christmas Stocking, Matthew Price

LANGUAGE/THINKING SKILLS:: Today you are going to make the body of Santa. You will make the head at another center, if you haven't already made one. How would you describe Santa's body? (big, fat tummy, covered with a red suit, etc.) What does his suit of clothes look like? (red with fur, a belt and buttons) What does he wear on his feet? (black boots with a fur trim) Our Santas will be fat and jolly looking, just like the one we see in story books.

PROCEDURES: MODEL EACH STEP CAREFULLY.
1. Have children cut out all three red, dittoed, 8" circles.
2. For the belt, take the 8" X 1 1/2" black rectangle and paste in the center of the whole red circle.
3. For fur on belt, take the 8" X 1 1/2" white rectangle and make it look "furry" by cutting in and out. Paste on bottom of belt.
4. Paste white 2 1/2" square in middle of the belt, paste black 2" square on top of the white to form the belt buckle.
5. Use two white 2 1/2" squares for buttons, cutting in and out to give a furry or lumpy look.
6. For legs, take an 8" red circle and fold in half like a taco then cut on the fold. Paste legs to the under side of the body.
7. Cut out pre-traced boots and use the 4" X 1" rectangles for the fur on the boots. Cut in and out for a "furry" look. Paste on tops of boots and trim off ends if necessary.
8. For arms, take the last 8" red circle and fold like a taco. This time, do not cut on the fold. Instead, while still folded, cut about 1" from the fold line. Paste to the back of the body.
9. Cut our pre-traced mittens and cut 4" X 1" rectangles into fur trim. Paste on top edge of mittens. Put names on back and attach to Santa's head, if that has been completed. Set aside to dry.

SANTA'S SLEIGH - COOKING

APPROXIMATE TIME: 20 minutes

OBJECTIVES - Students will:
1. develop auditory skills by following step-by-step directions.
2. practice math concept of dividing in half.
3. use language skills to discuss Santa's sleigh.

MATERIALS PER CLASS OF 32
1. Sixteen frozen waffle squares
2. Peanut butter and/or red jelly
3. Thirty-two teddy grahams for Santa
4. Thirty-two potato chips for Santa's bag.
5. Eight bananas for runners of sleigh.
6. One toaster
7. Knives for spreading peanut butter
8. Paper plates
9. Optional - licorice strings for reins

SUGGESTED LITERATURE:
   The Night Before Christmas, Clement Moore

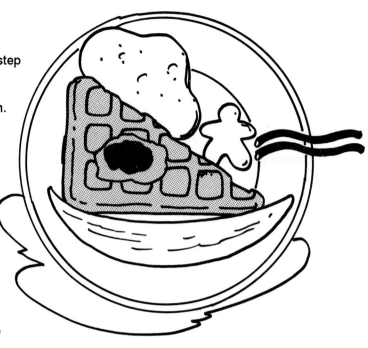

LANGUAGE/THINKING SKILLS:
What do we call the vehicle that Santa rides in when he delivers presents? (sleigh) What does a sleigh look like? (accept answers) Why does a sleigh have runners instead of wheels? (because it lands on snow) Would you like to ride in Santa's sleigh? Why? Today you are going to make a Santa sleigh that you can eat!

PROCEDURES FOR GROUP OF EIGHT STUDENTS:
1. Place 4 squares of frozen waffles in the toaster.
2. While waffles are toasting, help students take turns cutting a banana lengthwise into 4 pieces.
3. Pass out paper plates and spreading knives.
4. Cut each square waffle diagonally to make two triangles. Give each child a triangle.
5. Spread peanut butter and/or red jelly on triangle for paint.
6. Place potato chip in back of sleigh for Santa's present bag.
7. Place Teddy Graham in front of sleigh to simulate Santa.
8. Place banana on bottom for sleigh runner.
9. Use licorice string for reins if desired.
10. Eat and enjoy!
11. Have children help up clean the center.

RUDOLPH THE RED NOSED REINDEER

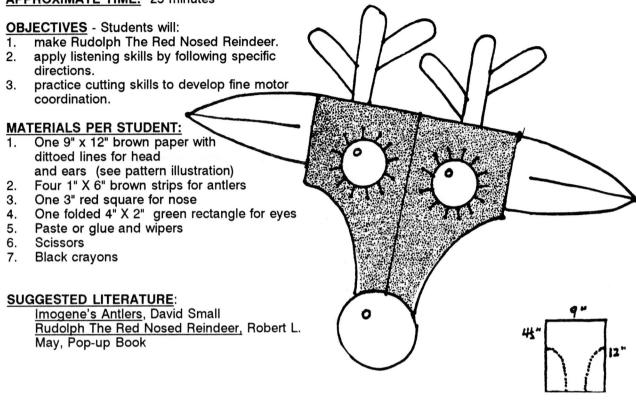

APPROXIMATE TIME: 25 minutes

OBJECTIVES - Students will:
1. make Rudolph The Red Nosed Reindeer.
2. apply listening skills by following specific directions.
3. practice cutting skills to develop fine motor coordination.

MATERIALS PER STUDENT:
1. One 9" x 12" brown paper with dittoed lines for head and ears (see pattern illustration)
2. Four 1" X 6" brown strips for antlers
3. One 3" red square for nose
4. One folded 4" X 2" green rectangle for eyes
5. Paste or glue and wipers
6. Scissors
7. Black crayons

SUGGESTED LITERATURE:
Imogene's Antlers, David Small
Rudolph The Red Nosed Reindeer, Robert L. May, Pop-up Book

LANGUAGE/THINKING SKILLS: How many reindeer did Santa have? (9) What were some of their names? (Dasher, Dancer, Prancer, Blitzen, Comet, Cupid, Donder, Vixen, Rudolph) Which one had the red shiny nose? (Rudolph) What did he do with his nose? (Guided the way for Santa's sleigh.) Today we are going to make Rudolph with his big shiny red nose. (Show children the sample and point out that the nose is very large.)

PROCEDURES:
1. Pass out large brown paper with ditto lines and tell children to cut on the lines and save the pieces for ears.
2. Paste the ears to the wide part of the head keeping flat side on top. (The ears may be pasted at various angles if the children wish.)
3. Give children a red square and tell them to make it into a circle by rounding off the corners, keeping the circle as large as possible.
4. Turn the paper so the ears are pasted to the back of the head, then paste the red circle to the bottom of the nose.
5. Give each child a folded green rectangle for the eyes. Have them cut a circle by rounding the corners. Paste the circle eyes to the head.
6. Pass out 2 brown strips to each child, and have them place them on top of each other and round one end to form the longest antler.
7. Now pass out 2 more brown strips; place them on top of each other and fold in half. Cut on the fold and round one end of each piece. This will make 4 short antlers to be pasted to each long antler. Paste both antlers to the back of the deer head.
8. Use a black crayon to make eyelashes and pupils on the eyes.
9. When dry, fold nose lengthwise to give it dimension.
10. Put names on back and have children help clean up the center.

QUILLING CHRISTMAS ORNAMENT

APPROXIMATE TIME: 25 minutes

OBJECTIVES - Students will:
1. make a beautiful Christmas ornament.
2. apply listening skills by following specific directions.
3. decorate the classroom or tree for the holiday.
4. practice new art techniques using paper and glue.
5. express feelings of pride in a finished product.

MATERIALS PER STUDENT:
1. Eight 1/2" X 1" strips of several different colors of paper (Astrobrite is the best, but colored butcher paper or a light weight construction paper will do.)
2. White glue
3. Paper punch and short string for hanging
4. Large primary pencils for curling
5. Moistened hand wipers
6. Paper to cover tables

SUGGESTED LITERATURE:
   Wake Up, Bear, It's Christmas, Stephen Gammel

LANGUAGE/THINKING SKILLS: Today we are going to make something that you might not believe you can do. (show sample) How many of you think this looks like it would be hard to make? What do you think it might be called? Some people call it quilling but we're going to call it a fancy ornament. I'm going to show you exactly what to do as we work. Are you ready?

PROCEDURES:
1. First, choose four strips of your favorite color.
2. Adult puts a line of glue on the covered table in front of each child. (Squeeze the line of glue just above child's working area)
3. Take one strip of paper and lightly touch one of the ends in the glue and make a raindrop. Do the same with the other three strips.
4. Now we are going to make eyeglasses like this. Dip the rounded end of the raindrop in the glue and press it together.
5. This time we are going to add another raindrop to form a bonfire.
6. Now we will add the last raindrop to make a star like this.
7. Now choose 4 strips of one other color. (hand out pencils) Curl the strips by wrapping them tightly around the pencil. Slide it off the pencil and hold on tightly for the next step.
8. Dip the outside edge of the rolled circle in the glue and place it in the wide end of the raindrop. It will spring, and the children will love the "boings." Continue adding "boings" to the other raindrops making sure the pattern is balanced.
9. Complete by punching a hole and hanging by any length string. Put names on somewhere. No one will believe children made these!

SALT DOUGH ORNAMENT

APPROXIMATE TIME: 25 minutes

OBJECTIVES - Students will:
1. roll out dough.
2. use cookie cutters to make tree ornaments.
3. practice cooperative sharing with their classmates.
4. follow specific directions to increase their listening skills.

MATERIALS PER GROUP OF 8 STUDENTS:
1. Two batches of salt dough in selected colors (See recipe at the bottom of the page. You'll need flour, cornstarch, plain salt, and liquid or paste food coloring.
2. Rolling pins or straight-sided plastic glasses (such as Tupperware) to roll out dough
3. Extra flour to avoid sticking
4. Several Christmas cookie cutters to share
5. Cookie sheet and spatula
6. Aluminum foil and felt tip marker
7. Oven

SUGGESTED LITERATURE:
    Max's Christmas, Rosemary Wells

LANGUAGE/THINKING SKILLS: Have you ever helped roll out cookie dough and then used cookie cutters like these? (show cutters) What did you make? Did you eat them? Today we are going to roll out some special dough, called salt dough. It's not good to eat but it's great for making Christmas ornaments. After the dough is baked in an oven, it will become hard and you can hang them on a Christmas tree or give your ornaments to someone special for a gift.

PROCEDURES: Cover the tables with white butcher paper, shiny side up.
1. Have each child write his/her name on the paper in front of him/her, out of the immediate work area.
2. Sprinkle a handful of flour on each child's working area.
3. Divide the batches of dough to equal the number of students in the group plus a share for the helping adult to use for demonstration. Sprinkle a small amount of flour on working area.
4. Model how to roll the dough, applying pressure evenly, until it is about 1/4" thick. Then flour a cookie cutter and cut a shape. Using the end of a paper clip, poke a fair-sized hole in the top.
5. Distribute rolling devices and let children roll the dough, then cut as many shapes as their dough allows. Help them poke holes.
6. Using a spatula, place the ornaments on a foil-covered cookie sheet. Write each child's name on the foil with a felt tip marker and draw a ring around his/her ornaments.
7. Have the children wash the cutters and clean the center.
8. Bake at 250 degrees for approximately 1 hour or until hard. Allow to cool in the oven before removing.

SALT DOUGH RECIPE: Mix thoroughly, sifting once: 1 cup flour, 1/2 cup cornstarch, 1/2 cup salt (plain not iodized). Add 1/2 cup water to mixture. (additional water may be needed) Knead dough for 5 minutes or until smooth. Add food coloring, store in sealed plastic container or bag.

POPCORN AND MACARONI CHAIN

APPROXIMATE TIME: 25 minutes

OBJECTIVES - Students will:
1. count popcorn and complete a math patterning activity.
2. apply fine motor skills by using a needle and thread to string popcorn.
3. discuss a holiday tradition from the past.
4. decorate a classroom or home tree.

MATERIALS PER STUDENT:
1. One 30" strand of sturdy carpet thread, double threaded, and secured on the end with a piece of salad macaroni (Helpful hint: Hang threaded needles on the bulletin board to prevent tangling.)
2. Lots of popped fluffy white corn (Day old popcorn does not break as easily.)
3. Lots of dyed red macaroni (salad or mostaccioli macaroni)

RECIPE FOR COLORING MACARONI: (adult activity)
2 T. alcohol mixed with liquid food coloring and 1/2 lb. macaroni
Place in a large bowl and mix until the macaroni is desired color.

SUGGESTED LITERATURE:
  Night Tree, Eve Bunting

LANGUAGE/THINKING SKILLS: What do you use to decorate your Christmas tree? What do you think people used before they could buy pretty ornaments and lights? (candles, pine cones, homemade things like cookies, paper dolls) Sometimes they used strings of popcorn and cranberries. Today, we are going to string popcorn and use red dyed macaroni instead of cranberries. Cranberries would rot and fall off before Christmas Day. We are going to make patterns and after we decorate our tree with them, you may take the chains home to use on your home tree.

PROCEDURES: CAUTION CHILDREN ABOUT USING NEEDLES CAREFULLY AND BE SURE TO SHOW THEM HOW TO HOLD THE POPCORN SO THEY WON'T POKE THEIR FINGERS.
1. Give each child a threaded needle. Have them start their own patterns but encourage them to use at least 10 popcorn pieces before they put on a macaroni.
2. Continue making a pattern until time runs out. When finished, fold a piece of masking tape over the thread near the needle end and cut the thread above the tape. Write the child's name on the tape and pin to bulletin board until time to decorate the tree.
3. Have the children help clean the center.

CIRCLE ORNAMENT

APPROXIMATE TIME: 25 minutes

OBJECTIVES - Students will:
1. create an original design or picture on a circle.
2. discuss the meaning of the word "ornament."
3. practice coloring to achieve dark, vibrant colors.
4. learn to use glue and glitter as a new art technique.

MATERIALS PER STUDENT:
1. 5"-7" circle (inside of a paper plate saved from Christmas wreath activity)
2. Crayons
3. White glue
4. Glitter
5. Enough heavy yarn to go around the outside edge of each circle, cut to length
6. Pictures of ornaments or actual round ornaments (optional)

SUGGESTED LITERATURE:
   The Little Fir Tree, Margaret Wise Brown

LANGUAGE/THINKING SKILLS: Who knows what an ornament is? (a decoration, something to beautify) Are all ornaments alike? (no) Are all ornaments round? (no) What time of year is it when we usually think about ornaments? (Christmas) What do ornaments look like? Do they have pictures on them or patterns? (Generate descriptive language, then show samples or pictures of real ornaments.) Even though we see many tree ornaments at Christmas time, ornaments are also used all year in many of your homes to decorate or make your homes more beautiful. Can anyone think of an ornament at your home that stays out all year long? (Accept all answers pertaining to home decorations.) Today we are going to make a circle ornament like many seen around holiday time.

PROCEDURES:
1. Pass out circles and crayons and ask children to write their names on the back.
2. Let children draw their designs or pictures. Encourage them to cover all the white areas and color darkly for more bright colors.
3. Next put down a large piece of paper to catch excess glitter.
4. Place the child's ornament on the paper, and adult uses white glue to outline parts of the design.
5. Child sprinkles glitter on white glue then picks up the ornament, and gently taps the side on the paper to remove excess glitter.
6. When glitter is in place, adult squeezes white glue around the outside edge of the circle.
7. Show children how to take a piece of colored yarn, start at one end and gently place the yarn on top of the glue to frame their ornament. Pass out yarn and help children as needed.
8. Set ornament aside to dry.
9. Have children help clean center, putting extra glitter back in jar.

CHRISTMAS WREATH

APPROXIMATE TIME: Two 25 minute periods with discussion and clean-up, or one 40 minute period

OBJECTIVES - Students will:
1. discuss different holiday decorations.
2. make a tissue paper wreath.
3. practice new art technique of making tissue flowers.
4. practice working cooperatively in a group situation.

MATERIALS PER STUDENT:
1. Approximately 30 dark green and 30 light green 3 1/2" tissue squares
2. One 9" hollowed out, sturdy paper plate (save circle center for the Circle Ornament project)
3. Soft wire or string to hang wreath
4. Paste or glue and wipe clothes
5. Ten or twelve red 1/2" squares for berries
6. One red yarn bow
7. Sample of completed project

SUGGESTED LITERATURE:
   The Night Before Christmas, Clement Moore

LANGUAGE/THINKING SKILLS: (show sample) What is this pretty holiday decoration called? (wreath) Where might you see one at holiday time? (They are on doors, fireplaces or in stores.) Are they usually made of tissue paper? What things from nature might be used to make a wreath? (evergreens and holly berries) Have you ever seen a wreath made of something else? (Some people make them out of cloth or bare vines.) Today we are going to make one like this sample by using tissue paper and paper plates with the center circle cut out.

PROCEDURES: IF MAKING IN TWO SESSIONS, MAKE THE TISSUE FLOWERS DURING THE FIRST SESSION, AND SAVE TO COMPLETE DURING THE SECOND SESSION.
1. Model how to make a tissue flower by making a circle with your thumb and index finger and placing a tissue square over the hole. Next using the index finger of your other hand, push the tissue gently through the hole and pinch and twist the bottom. Another technique is to push up around finger and twist on the bottom.
2. When at least 20 are made, spread paste or glue heavily around the outside edge for about a 4 inch space, and press the flowers on so that all of the white plate is hidden.
3. Continue making flowers and pasting until the entire white wreath is covered. It will take perseverance and you may need to assist the slower workers.
4. After wreath is covered, have the children cut the red squares into circles by rounding off the corners. Paste the berries randomly around the wreath.
5. Adult - Poke hole with a sharp object and string with a wire loop. Put a dab of glue opposite the hanger and have the child press the ribbon into the glue, holding for a count of ten.

CHRISTMAS PACKAGE PLACEMAT

APPROXIMATE TIME: 25 minutes

OBJECTIVES - Students will:
1. practice fine motor skills by tracing and cutting objects.
2. create uniquely designed packages.
3. make a placemat for Christmas party or for use as a room decoration.

MATERIALS PER STUDENT:
1. One 9" X 18" red construction paper
2. Two 18" X 1/2" white strips to simulate ribbon
3. A variety of patterns to trace or copy (see pattern illustrations)
4. Construction paper rectangles and squares of various sizes and colors (large enough to trace patterns)
5. Pencils
6. Paste or glue
7. Scissors

SUGGESTED LITERATURE:
The Polar Express, Chris Van Allsburg

LANGUAGE/THINKING SKILLS: What kinds of things do people often place under trees at Christmas time? (packages) What do they look like? (brightly wrapped) Today we are going to make placemats that look like beautifully wrapped packages. We are going to use paper strips for ribbons and we are going to trace different decorations to put on our packages. Look at the patterns that you might like to trace, cut out, and put on your placemat. How do you want your package placemat to look?

PROCEDURES: BE SURE TO MODEL THE TRACING OF PATTERNS, OR THEY WILL GLUE YOUR PATTERNS TO THEIR PACKAGES RATHER THAN TRACE AND CUT THEIR OWN.
1. Show the children the various ways that the white "ribbons" can be put on packages. Put paste or glue on the back of the "ribbons" and place them on the "package."

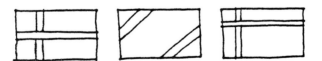

2. Hold up the various pattern templates or choices and let them select the one they wish and the color of paper they wish to trace the pattern upon. They may trace and cut as many as time permits.
3. Glue traced patterns to the "package."
4. When completed, put names on the back of the placemat package and save for the party or for room decoration.
5. Have the children help clean up the center.

CHRISTMAS COUNTDOWN CHAIN

APPROXIMATE TIME: 25 minutes

OBJECTIVES - Students will:
1. apply listening skills by following specific directions.
2. review the concept of days and weeks.
3. assemble a 1 to 1 math patterning activity.
4. practice counting objects.

MATERIALS PER STUDENT:
1. Seven 1" x 9" red strips
2. Seven 1" X 9" green strips
3. One 1" X 9" yellow strip
4. Paste or glue
5. Lunch size paper bag
6. Christmas countdown poem (included)
7. Ditto of activity directions to include in child's bag

DID YOUR CHILD FOLLOW DIRECTIONS?
1. Is there a yellow loop on one end?
2. Are there 7 red and 7 green strips?
3. Is there a red, green pattern?
4. Is there a total of 15 links?

SUGGESTED LITERATURE:
 The Twelve Days of Christmas, Jan Brett

LANGUAGE/THINKING SKILLS: How many days do you think it is until Christmas? (Use the calendar to count, if necessary.) How many days are in one week? (Name the days of week and count them.) Then, how many weeks until Christmas? Today we are going to make a countdown paper chain to help us keep track of how many days are left until Christmas. This chain will hang up with the yellow loop on top, and each day you can take off one loop from the bottom. When you reach the yellow loop, it will be Christmas day.

PROCEDURES: BE SURE TO EMPHASIZE THE IMPORTANCE OF MAKING A PATTERN.
1. Read the poem below to the group first, then place the colored strips in the middle of the table and have each person count 7 red strips, 7 green strips, and 1 yellow strip.
2. Start with the yellow strip, and have them roll it and paste it to make a loop. Tell them that this yellow loop will always be on one end, never between any other colors.
3. Next take a red strip and interlock with the yellow strip to form the beginning of a chain. Continue alternating the red and green strips to make a pattern.
4. Place the completed chain in a paper bag along with the poem and the ditto saying, "DID YOUR CHILD FOLLOW DIRECTIONS?"

MY CHRISTMAS CHAIN

Christmas Day will soon be here, and I can hardly wait.
I've made this little countdown chain to help me celebrate.
Each day I'll snip one loop from it, to help me to remember.
That merry, merry Christmas Day is the 25th of December.
Please help me hang my chain up high, I'll cut one loop each day.
And when I reach the yellow loop, it will be Merry Christmas Day!

GRAHAM CRACKER HOUSE

APPROXIMATE TIME: 45 minutes

OBJECTIVES - Students will:
1.   make a Gingerbread House.
2.   apply listening skills by following specific directions.
3.   recall part of the story of Hansel and Gretel.
4.   experiment with using pastry tubes.

MATERIALS PER STUDENT:
1.   One foil wrapped heavy piece of cardboard for base - 8" X 10"
2.   Four rectangle graham crackers
3.   Two previously cut pointed graham crackers (You need a sharp knife on a flat surface to cut successfully. Prepare extras for breakage.)
4.   One paper pastry tube filled half-way with white frosting (see recipe)
     Paper pastry tubes can be purchased at a cake decorating store where they will show you how to fold them.
5.   One cup brightly colored cereal or raisins
6.   One plastic knife

FROSTING RECIPE
3 level T. Meringue powder
4 C. sifted powdered sugar
1/4 C. plus 2 T. water

Beat on low speed for 7 - 10 minutes until stiff peaks form.
1 recipe per 3 students

SUGGESTED LITERATURE:
   <u>Hansel and Gretel</u>, Paul O. Zelinsky
   (or use your favorite Hansel and Gretel book)

LANGUAGE/THINKING SKILLS:: How many of you have seen Gingerbread houses before? What time of the year would you usually see one? (Christmas) Why is there white frosting on them? (to look like snow) Do you remember hearing a story about a woman who lived in a Gingerbread house? (Hansel and Gretel) Remember what they did when they saw it? (They took bites of it.) Today we are going to make Gingerbread houses out of graham crackers, and instead of eating them, we're going to use them to decorate our classroom, and then your house!

PROCEDURES: Assemble the four sides of the house, one at a time, by following these directions.
1.   Squeeze a thick rectangle of frosting on the foil base. Make it the length of a rectangle graham cracker and the width of the pointed graham cracker.
2.   Squeeze a thick line of frosting onto the vertical edges of the pointed cracker (not the roof area yet) and press in gently into the frosting base. Hold for a minute, then gently place the rectangular cracker into the frosting, overlapping the pointed cracker at the corner. Hold until firm. (Do not rush.)
3.   Repeat step #2 for the remaining sides, placing the pointed cracker in place first so that it's just inside the side panels.
4.   Squeeze a line of frosting around all of the top edges.
5.   Place one rectangular cracker on top for the roof, Hold for a minute, then gently place the other roof cracker. (The roof pieces will not fit perfectly.) Let it set up for a few minutes.
6.   Squeeze frosting back and forth over the roof opening and on the edges of the roof.
7.   Gently decorate with cereal. If desired, use small pieces of graham cracker for doors and shutters and adhere with frosting.
8.   Squeeze any extra frosting around the base to look like snow.

HANUKKAH - A SPECIAL HOLIDAY

Everyone loves holidays because they are special times to get together with relatives, eat special foods, and celebrate! The Jewish people celebrate a special holiday called Hanukkah at almost the same time of year as many celebrate Christmas. The Jewish people are remembering a victory that was won many years ago. Their temple, or church, was taken over by the enemy and they had to fight to get it back. Part of the temple was destroyed, and it had to be rebuilt. While they were cleaning up their temple, they found only one small container of lamp oil which they could use to light their Holy lamp but it was only enough to burn for one day. The people were very surprised and happy when a miracle happened, and the lamp burned for eight whole days! Today, many Jewish people celebrate Hanukkah by lighting a Menorah. This is a candle holder for 9 candles. (show picture) The candle in the middle stands for the flame that burned so long ago. It is used to light the other eight candles, one a night, for eight nights. During Hanukkah, gifts are exchanged and special foods are prepared. One of these foods is called Potato Latkes which are like potato pancakes. They can be eaten plain or served with applesauce and sour cream. A popular game, The Dreidel Game, is also played during the Hanukkah celebration. (See activity for Potato Latkes and for The Dreidel Game.)

THE DREIDEL GAME

APPROXIMATE TIME: 20 minutes

OBJECTIVES - Students will:
1. learn a new game played at the holidays by Jewish families to celebrate Hanukkah.
2. practice counting through game activities.
3. practice taking turns and being good sports in a cooperative group game.

MATERIALS PER GROUP:
1. One copy of the directions and explanations of symbols for the adult at the center
2. One dreidel
3. Markers for each child (beans, chips etc.)

SUGGESTED LITERATURE:
My First Hanukkah Book, Aileen Fisher

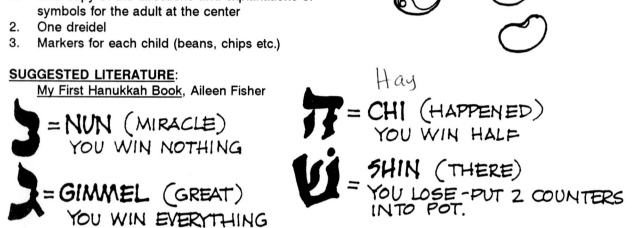

ℶ = NUN (MIRACLE)
YOU WIN NOTHING

ℷ = GIMMEL (GREAT)
YOU WIN EVERYTHING

Hay
ℸ = CHI (HAPPENED)
YOU WIN HALF

ש = SHIN (THERE)
YOU LOSE - PUT 2 COUNTERS INTO POT.

LANGUAGE/THINKING SKILLS: (Review or introduce Hanukkah as previously described. A dreidel is a type of top used to play a game. (show dreidel) It has symbols on the sides. The symbols stand for "A great miracle happened there." (note symbols above) Each player is given 10 - 15 markers to play the game. It is a favorite game of the Jewish people because it reminds them of the time the Holy oil lamp burned for 8 days when it only had enough oil to burn for one day. That was a miracle or something which everyone thought was impossible.

PROCEDURES: This game is best when played by only four at a time.
1. Give each player 10 to 15 markers.
2. Each player puts 2 markers in the center of the playing area. (The center area is known as the kitty.)
3. The first player (could be the youngest) spins the dreidel. The Hebrew letter which shows on top tells what that player should do.
   (See above symbols.)
4. When the "kitty" is empty or there is only one marker left, each player puts in 2 more markers.
5. When one player has won everything, the game is over.
6. If an off number is in the "kitty", (example - 3) and "hay" is rolled, the player takes half plus one more. (example - 2)

HAVE FUN !

POTATO LATKES - COOKING

APPROXIMATE TIME: 30 - 35 minutes

OBJECTIVES - Students will:
1. prepare a traditional Jewish recipe.
2. learn new vocabulary words such as Menorah, Hanukkah, Jewish, and grate
3. participate in a discussion of the Jewish holiday, Hanukkah.

MATERIALS PER GROUP OF 8 CHILDREN:
1. Grater or food processor
2. Electric frying pan
3. Paper towels
4. Metal spatula and potato peelers
5. Knives (pumpkin cutters work well)
6. Paper plates and forks
7. Ingredients for recipe (see below)

INGREDIENTS FOR 8 CHILDREN: 4 peeled potatoes, 1 small peeled onion, 1 egg, 1 T. flour, 1 1/2 tsp. salt, and a little salad oil. Applesauce and sour cream (optional)

SUGGESTED LITERATURE:
  Potato Pancakes All Around, Marilyn Hirsh

LANGUAGE/THINKING SKILLS: (Review or introduce the holiday, Hanukkah. See Hanukkah information and read it to the children if they have not already heard the story or if they are unclear about the meaning.) When you heard the story of Hanukkah, it mentioned that a popular food eaten during the holiday celebration is Potato Latkes or potato pancakes. Today we are going to make this food and eat it. We will all cooperate to make this tasty recipe.

PROCEDURES:
1. Have all children wash their hands.
2. Adult cuts the onion and potatoes in half so that each child may grate one or take turns pushing the feed tube into the food processor if one is used.
3. Pre-heat the frying pan and add oil. KEEP OUT OF CHILDREN'S REACH!
4. Place grated potatoes and onions in a bowl and have children take turns adding the flour, salt and egg.
5. Divide the mixture into 8-9 servings and give each child a serving amount to make into a pancake shape.
6. Adult - place the pancakes into the hot oil and fry until golden brown. While waiting, discuss Hanukkah, Christmas, their holiday plans, their wish lists, whether they have visited Santa, etc.
7. Drain the pancakes on paper towels.
8. While still warm, serve with applesauce and sour cream (optional)
9. Have children clean up their own plates, and place the dirty forks in a designated area.

WINTER

SHAVING CREAM DESIGNS AND PRINTS

APPROXIMATE TIME: 25 minutes

OBJECTIVES - Students will:
1. participate in a tactile art experience.
2. experiment with and create several original designs in shaving cream.
3. make a print of a "snow" scene.
4. practice cooperative play.

MATERIALS PER GROUP OF 8 STUDENTS:
1. 1/2 - large can of shaving cream
2. Tables for working area
3. Paint aprons for each student
4. One large bath towel for clean up or 1 washcloth per child
5. Sixteen pieces of blue Astrobrite paper for making prints

SUGGESTED LITERATURE:
   First Snow, Emily McCully

LANGUAGE/THINKING SKILLS: How many of you have ever played in real snow? Today we are going to pretend that shaving cream is snow. I'll spray it right on the table in front of you, and you can make any kind of design that you wish. What are some things that you could make? (snowmen, valentines, dinosaurs, self-portraits, a flag, or any other creative idea) When you have made a picture that you like, you can save it by making a print of it. This is done by carefully pressing a paper on your design and lifting it off. While you are making your picture, we will describe the fragrance of shaving cream.

PROCEDURES
1. Put on paint aprons.
2. Adult should shake can and spray a mound of shaving cream right on the table in front of the student.
3. Children should work with the shaving cream for several minutes, just for pure enjoyment. Printmaking can begin when most of the bubbles disappear.
4. When a child has created a design or picture he/she likes, help him position the paper over it, then he/she should press lightly and lift off gently.
5. Carefully put names on paper and set aside to dry.
6. New designs can be created as time allows. Add more shaving cream if necessary.
7. Have children help clean up the area with a large damp towel.

SNOWFLAKES

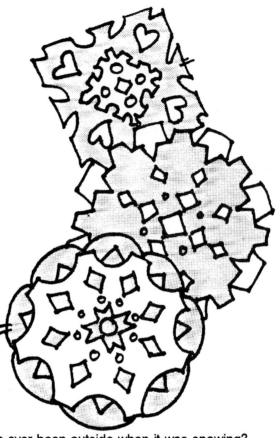

APPROXIMATE TIME: 25 minutes

OBJECTIVES - Students will:
1. cut pre-folded paper to make snowflakes.
2. learn how to fold paper for cutting into snowflakes.
3. create their own snowflake designs by learning to make different cuts.

MATERIALS PER STUDENT:
1. Several pre-folded 8" and 6" squares of light blue and white typing or mimeograph paper.
2. Several unfolded 8" and 6" squares of light blue and white typing or mimeograph paper.
3. Scissors
4. Pencils for writing names on snowflakes

SUGGESTED LITERATURE:
Snow is Falling, Franklyn M. Branley

LANGUAGE/THINKING SKILLS: How many of you have ever been outside when it was snowing? (responses) Have you ever caught a snowflake? Can anyone describe what a snowflake looks like? (responses) Did you know that snowflakes are tiny crystals of frozen water? When they fall from the sky, they float like tiny feathers to the ground. If you have ever seen some fall on your clothes, you may have noticed that each one is shaped differently. If you could look at one under a microscope, you would see that each one has six sides. Today we are going to make paper snowflakes, and we will make each one different. To make them easier to cut, our paper snowflakes will have only four sides.

PROCEDURES:
1. Show children how to fold the square to make a triangle. Fold that triangle in half to form another triangle, then in half again.
2. Show children how to cut any shape hole in the sides and points, being careful not to cut off all the folded edge. Show them how they can cut the side opposite the point to create a different edge.
3. The children should have adult check their work before they open up the snowflake. The tendency is to make too few cuts and the paper is difficult to refold. Encourage them to make several cuts before opening up the snowflake. (If children cannot cut through all the thicknesses, have them eliminate one fold.) It looks nice to paste small snowflake on a larger one of the contrasting color.
4. Have children put their names on each one and continue as long as time permits.
5. Have children help clean up the area.

PAIR OF MITTENS

APPROXIMATE TIME: 25 MINUTES

OBJECTIVES - Students will:
1. make a matching pair of mittens.
2. discuss the concept of "pair."
3. create a mirror image pattern.
4. become aware of "left" and "right."
5. practice cutting on curved lines.

MATERIALS PER STUDENT
1. One pair of dittoed mittens on manilla construction paper (see pattern illustration)
2. Crayons
3. One 24" piece of string or yarn
4. Scotch tape or masking tape
5. Samples of real, patterned mittens
6. Small hand mirror

SUGGESTED LITERATURE:
   The Mitten, Alvin Tresselt

LANGUAGE/THINKING SKILLS: When we have a pair of something, we have two things that are alike. Can anyone think of some things that come in pairs? (shoes, socks, mittens, gloves, etc.) What is the difference between a pair of gloves and a pair of mittens? (Gloves have separate places for the fingers, mittens do not.) Today we are going to make a pair of mittens. (Show samples of mittens. Mix them up and see if children can match the pairs.) How did you know which ones went together? Look carefully at the designs on the mittens. Are all mittens alike? (no) What could you make on your mittens? (tree, snowman, etc.) Let's all try to make our mitten designs different from our neighbor's.

PROCEDURES
1. Using a mirror and a pair of patterned mittens, show children what happens when the mirror is placed between the mittens. (A mirror image occurs. Children will see the pattern repeated in mirror.)
2. Show children how to use a dark crayon to outline the mittens.
3. Pass out dittoed mittens, and have children outline mittens as demonstrated.
4. Have children place the pair of mittens in front of them and instruct them that in order to make a mirror image, they should draw something on one mitten, and then immediately draw the same thing on the other mitten. Continue working until the entire mittens are covered with matching designs.
5. Instruct children to cut out the mittens carefully.
6. Attach strings to the backs of the mittens with tape.
7. Have children match their right and left hands to the right and left mittens, then put their names on the back of both mittens.

SNOW CONES - COOKING

APPROXIMATE TIME: 25 minutes

OBJECTIVES - Students will:
1. make "snow" out of ice.
2. make grape juice from frozen concentrate.
3. use "winter vocabulary" to discuss what their mouths feel like when eating snow cones. (cold, freezing, icy, frigid, etc.)
4. participate in a cooperative cooking project.

MATERIALS PER GROUP OF 8 STUDENTS:
1. Snow cone machine or crushed ice maker or food processor
2. A large bowl of small ice cubes or crushed ice
3. 1 - 12 oz. can of frozen grape juice
4. Water
5. Small cups and spoons
6. Pitcher for diluted grape juice

SUGGESTED LITERATURE:
 Snowy Day, Ezra Jack Keats

LANGUAGE/THINKING SKILLS: Has anyone ever eaten real snow? (responses) What did it taste like? (cold, icy, frigid, freezing, etc.) What happened to it when you put it in your mouth? (it melted, turned into water, etc.) Why did it melt in your mouth? (Because your mouth is warm, anything that is frozen will melt when placed in your mouth.) Today we are going to make grape snow cones by crushing ice and pouring grape juice over it. Then we will see what happens when we eat the snow cones, and we will talk about how the ice feels in our mouths.

PROCEDURES
1. Demonstrate how to use the ice crusher or snow cone machine.
2. Let each child take a turn at making the "snow" from the ice cubes or crushed ice. (Since this is time consuming, you may wish to supplement with some pre-made "snow" which has been kept in a freezer.
3. Add 1 can of water to the frozen juice concentrate.
4. When everyone has a cup of "snow," pour some grape juice over the ice, pass out the spoons, and eat and enjoy.
5. When the children first put the "snow" in their mouths, ask them to use words to describe what they feel in their mouths.
6. After the discussion, while the children are eating, read a winter or snow story to them.
7. Have the children help clean up the area.

WHIPPED SOAP SNOWMAN

APPROXIMATE TIME: 25 minutes

OBJECTIVES - Students will:
1. make artificial "snow" by whipping Ivory Snow.
2. create a whipped soap snowman to emphasize the winter season.
3. discuss the likenesses and differences of artificial snow and real snow.

MATERIALS PER 8 STUDENTS:
1. Large box of Ivory Snow soap per 16 students and water
2. Electric beater and large bowl
3. White powdered tempera paint
4. Eight 9" X 12" blue construction paper
5. A variety of construction paper scraps or buttons, pebbles, sticks, pipe cleaners, etc. for the snowman's eyes, nose, mouth, hat, scarf and pipe
6. Scissors
7. White glue
8. Paint aprons

SUGGESTED LITERATURE:
    Midnight Snowman, Caroline Feller Bauer

LANGUAGE/THINKING SKILLS: In what season of the year do we usually make snowmen and go skiing and sledding? (winter) How many of you have ever made or seen a snowman? (responses) What did you use other than snow to make him look like a snowman? (hat, eyes, nose, mouth, scarf, buttons, sticks for arms, etc.) Today we are going to make a snowman picture using pretend snow which we will make by beating Ivory Snow and water together. In what ways do you think it will look like real snow? (It will be white, fluffy, and we'll be able to hold it in our hands, and make something with it.) In what ways do you think it will be different from real snow? (It will not be cold, it will not melt, we will not be able to see separate flakes and it will have a fragrance.) After we make the "snow", you will be able to make a snowman on a piece of paper and decorate it any way you wish by using colored paper, buttons, sticks and pebbles.

PROCEDURES BE SURE AND COVER TABLES WITH PAPER.
1. Have children put on paint aprons.
2. Pour the Ivory Snow into a large bowl. Add the water a little at a time. (If you want a true white color, add a little powdered white tempera paint to the soap before mixing.) Beat at high speed until the suds stiffen into peaks.
3. Let each child use fingers to dip out about 1/4 cup for the bottom ball of the snowman. Place it on the bottom of the paper and smear it around to form a circle.
4. Repeat the procedure for the other two balls and for some snow on the ground.
5. Let children be creative in using the objects to decorate their snowmen. Use white glue to attach objects to the snowmen.
6. Put names on the bottom, and have children help clean the area.

ESKIMO HEAD

APPROXIMATE TIME: 25 minutes

OBJECTIVES - Students will:
1. make the head part of an Eskimo.
2. discuss Eskimos and what they wear.
3. practice listening skills by following specific directions
4. practice cutting and pasting skills.

MATERIALS PER STUDENT
1. One dittoed white 8" circle for fur hat
2. One dittoed manilla 6" circle for face
3. Black and red crayons
4. Scissors
5. Paste or glue
6. Picture book about Eskimos

SUGGESTED LITERATURE:
   On Mothers Lap, Ann Herbert Scott

LANGUAGE/THINKING SKILLS: Who can tell something about Eskimos? (They live near the North Pole where it is very cold. Some hunt and fish for food, use dogs to pull their sleds over the frozen ground and wear parkas to keep warm) Many Eskimos live near the sea where they fish, catch whales and seals, and hunt caribou. The Eskimos often use the skin of the animals they hunt to make their clothing to keep them warm in a very cold climate. Their jackets are called parkas, and they have fur linings and hoods that keep them warm. Today we are going to make the head of an Eskimo who is wearing a fur-lined hood. We will make the body of the Eskimo at another time. Then we will glue the body and head together.

PROCEDURES
1. Pass out dittoed manilla circles for the head and have children cut them out.
2. Using a black crayon, model how to draw the hair, eyes and nose.
3. Using a red crayon, add the mouth.
4. Pass out the white dittoed circle and have children cut it out.
5. Paste the face to the center of the white circle by putting paste on the back of the manilla face.
6. Model how to fringe around the outside of the white circle to simulate fur. Do not fringe the section under the chin. (See above illustration)
7. Put names on back and save until body is made.
8. Have children help clean the center.

ESKIMO BODY

APPROXIMATE TIME: 25 minutes

OBJECTIVES - Students will:
1. make the body part of an Eskimo.
2. discuss Eskimo culture, where they live, what they eat, and what they wear.
3. use scissors and paste to develop fine motor skills.
4. practice listening skills by following specific directions.

MATERIALS PER STUDENT
1. One 9" X 12" brown paper for body
2. Four 3" X 6" brown rectangles for arms and legs
3. Two each pre-traced mittens and boots (see pattern illustrations)
4. One 3" X 9" white rectangle for fur
5. Four 3 1/2" X 1 1/2" white rectangles for boot and mitten fur
6. Black crayons
7. Paste or glue
8. Scissors

SUGGESTED LITERATURE:
Very Last First Time, Jan Andrews

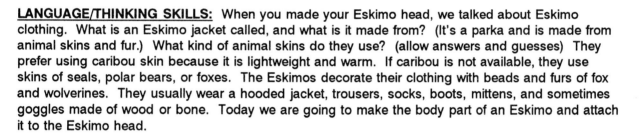

LANGUAGE/THINKING SKILLS: When you made your Eskimo head, we talked about Eskimo clothing. What is an Eskimo jacket called, and what is it made from? (It's a parka and is made from animal skins and fur.) What kind of animal skins do they use? (allow answers and guesses) They prefer using caribou skin because it is lightweight and warm. If caribou is not available, they use skins of seals, polar bears, or foxes. The Eskimos decorate their clothing with beads and furs of fox and wolverines. They usually wear a hooded jacket, trousers, socks, boots, mittens, and sometimes goggles made of wood or bone. Today we are going to make the body part of an Eskimo and attach it to the Eskimo head.

PROCEDURES
1. Pass out brown 9" X 12" and have children round shoulders.
2. Pass out 2 arms and 2 legs to each child. Model how they can arrange these to be waving, kicking, standing, etc. Paste or glue these to the body. Put name on this side, then turn over.
3. Cut out mittens and paste on the arms.
4. Cut out boots and paste on the legs.
5. Fringe large white rectangle on both sides to simulate fur. Paste on bottom of parka.
6. Fringe four small white rectangles for boot and mitten fur. (Have children cut two at a time.) Paste on boot and mitten edges.
7. Using a black crayon, have children make a zig-zag design on fur.
8. If head is completed, attach it to the body. Then using a black crayon, draw a rectangle under the chin and draw X's inside the rectangle to look like shoe laces.
9. Put names on back, and have children help clean the center.

ESKIMO IGLOO

APPROXIMATE TIME: 25 minutes

OBJECTIVES - Students will:
1. make an igloo out of white paper rectangles.
2. count out 18 rectangles or 1 set of 10 and 1 set of 8 rectangles for math counting practice.
3. practice proper use of paste.
4. discuss the housing of early Eskimos and compare and contrast it to their own present day housing.

MATERIALS PER STUDENT:
1. One 9" X 12" blue construction paper
2. Eighteen white rectangles 1" X 1 1/2"
3. One 1 1/2" X 2" black rectangle for tunnel entry
4. Paste or glue
5. White chalk

SUGGESTED LITERATURE:
 Alaska ABC Book, Charlene Kreeger and Shannon Cartwright

LANGUAGE/THINKING SKILLS: What kinds of houses do we think of when we think of early Eskimos? (Igloos) What are Igloos? (Igloos are any type of Eskimo housing, not just snowhouses. However, the type of house most often thought of as igloos are snowhouses.) How are igloos alike and different from our houses today? (responses) Eskimos often lived in remote areas where the hunting and fishing were good. In the winter they would often build snowhouses to live in, and in the summer they lived in tents. To build a snowhouse, it was necessary to locate firm ground and use the snow left by a single storm because layered snow blocks didn't hold together very well. Eskimos would use a swordlike knife to cut blocks of compacted snow. Each block was about 2 feet by 3 feet by 8 inches thick. Most igloos were about 12 feet high and 15 feet wide and were dome shaped. Today we are going to make paper igloos out of rectangles. We will make an entrance to remind us of the tunnel entrance the Eskimos made.

PROCEDURES
1. Place the cut rectangles in the middle of the table and have each child count out 18. If a child is unable to count that high, have him/her count out 1 set of 10 and 1 set of 8 for his/her igloo.
2. Pass out blue paper. Have children paste 6 rectangles along the bottom of the page, touching each other.
3. Take 5 rectangles and paste on the next row.
4. Take 4 rectangles and paste on the third row.
5. Take 3 rectangles and paste on the fourth row.
6. Take black rectangle and make a tunnel entry by rounding two of the corners and pasting on top of the "snow blocks."
8. Using white chalk, fill in the edges to make a dome shape.
9. Put names on the back, and have students clean the area.

PENGUIN

APPROXIMATE TIME: 25 minutes

OBJECTIVES - Students will:
1. make an Antarctic animal.
2. practice using vocabulary words such as Antarctica, iceberg, flippers, webbed and penguin in sentences.
3. practice cutting on curved lines.
4. practice listening skills by following specific directions.

MATERIALS PER STUDENT
1. One white paper bag (lunch size)
2. Newspapers for stuffing
3. Traced body and wings on black 9" X 12" paper (see pattern illustration)
4. Traced feet on black 9" X 3" black paper (see pattern illustration)
5. Two round gummed hole reinforcers for eyes
6. Scissors
7. Stapler
8. Paste or glue

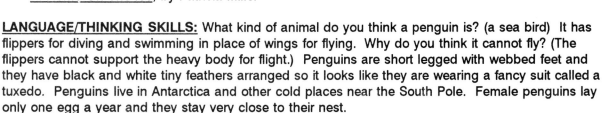

SUGGESTED LITERATURE:
Tacky the Penguin, Helen Lester
At Home On The Ice, by Patricia Miller

LANGUAGE/THINKING SKILLS: What kind of animal do you think a penguin is? (a sea bird) It has flippers for diving and swimming in place of wings for flying. Why do you think it cannot fly? (The flippers cannot support the heavy body for flight.) Penguins are short legged with webbed feet and they have black and white tiny feathers arranged so it looks like they are wearing a fancy suit called a tuxedo. Penguins live in Antarctica and other cold places near the South Pole. Female penguins lay only one egg a year and they stay very close to their nest.

PROCEDURES
1. Give each child a white paper bag. Put names on the bottom of the bag.
2. Have children tear small pieces of newspaper, wad them up, and put the newspaper balls in the bag until it is about 3/4 full.
3. Making sure that the flaps are on the seam side of the bag, adult folds corners of the top to make a triangle, and staples it.
4. Child cuts out the body and wing section, leaving it folded. (be careful cutting the beak line)
5. On the side of the white bag without seams, child spreads glue or paste only on the triangular top section.
6. Open up the cut body and wing section. Slip the beak section over the pasted area. The black body and wing sections hang loosely over the seamed side of the bag.
7. While still folded, cut out feet, and paste or glue to the bottom of the bag with the toes pointing outward.
8. Put white hole reinforcers on black face for eyes.
9. Have children clean the center area.

MARTIN LUTHER KING, JR.

DREAM

MARTIN LUTHER KING

Vera Refnes

Slow, Blues Style

Mar – tin Lu – ther King was such a kind and gen – tle man _____ He

had a dream that e – very one would car – ry out his plan. _____ He

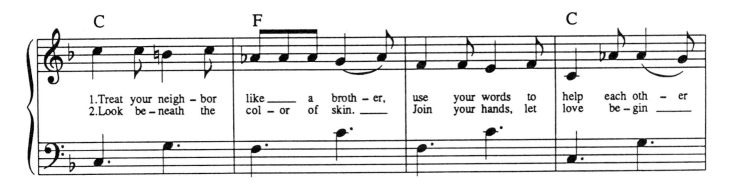

1. Treat your neigh – bor like _____ a broth – er, use your words to help each oth – er
2. Look be – neath the col – or of skin. _____ Join your hands, let love be – gin _____

Molto rit. - - - - - - - - - - - - 8 va

Mar – tin Lu – ther King was such a peace lov – in' man. _____

I HAVE A DREAM...

APPROXIMATE TIME: 25 minutes

OBJECTIVES - students will:
1. express their dreams for themselves, someone else and others.
2. discuss the life and dreams of a famous African American, Martin Luther King, Jr.
3. brainstorm ideas and create drawings to express ideas.

MATERIALS PER STUDENT:
1. One 12" x 18" white art paper labeled per illustration
2. Crayons

SUGGESTED LITERATURE:
   A Picture Book of Martin Luther King, Jr., David Adler

LANGUAGE/THINKING SKILLS: (Read about and discuss Martin Luther King, Jr. before beginning this project.) Martin Luther King was a man with a dream or hope for how things should be. He saw a problem and wanted to do something about it. Can anyone remember what problems worried King? (Black people and white people could not be together to be friends because they were treated differently.) He gave a speech in which he said he had a dream or hope that someday people of every color would live together happily, be kind to each other, and be allowed to do the same things. Do you have dreams or hopes too? What are some dreams or hopes you have for yourself? (to be happy, healthy, kind, helpful, etc.) What are some dreams you have for someone else? (my friend will get well, my dad will find a job, my family will find a good place to live, etc.) What about the world, do you have a dream or hope for the whole world? (no more drugs, no more wars, lots of trees and flowers, etc.) Today you are going to draw three pictures of your dreams and I will write the words that your picture says. Let's start with a dream for yourself.

PROCEDURES:
1. Pass out pre-marked papers, put a small x in pencil on the picture to do first.
2. Children will draw pictures of dreams for themselves while adult circulates and writes their descriptions on their papers.
3. Repeat procedures for other two dreams.
4. If time permits, share dreams with a partner.
5. Be sure children's names are on their papers.
6. Have children help put materials away.

SAND DINOSAURS

APPROXIMATE TIME: 25 minutes

OBJECTIVES - Students will:
1. draw original dinosaurs.
2. work with a new medium of diluted glue and "sand."
3. apply listening skills by following specific directions.

MATERIALS PER STUDENT:
1. One 12" X 18" white art paper
2. Pencil, paint brush, and paint apron
3. White glue
4. Dinosaur pictures
5. One plastic container of water diluted glue (1 to ratio) per two students
6. Large shirt box to catch "sand"
7. Pre-made "sand" of various colors

RECIPE FOR "SAND" (adult activity)
   2 cups white corn meal
   2 T rubbing alcohol mixed with food coloring
   Shake together in a jar or stir until colors blend.
   Spread to dry.

SUGGESTED LITERATURE:
   Dinosaurs Are Different, Aliki

LANGUAGE/THINKING SKILLS: Today you are going to create a very special dinosaur for our bulletin board. We don't really know what color dinosaurs were, so we can make any color. What kind of dinosaurs are your favorites? (allow responses) Let's look at dinosaur pictures to remind us of the different kinds. You may make any kind of dinosaur you wish, even one that no one has ever seen before.

PROCEDURES: MODEL EACH STEP BEFORE CHILDREN BEGIN.
1. Cover tables with white butcher paper and have children put on paint aprons.
2. Give each child a large piece of paper and a pencil.
3. Have children draw their favorite dinosaur and emphasize the importance of making it BIG so that it takes most of the paper.
4. Using white glue, adult will trace over child's pencil lines.
5. Child takes glue outlined drawing to a box and sprinkles "sand" over the glue, shakes it off and lifts it from box. The "sand" will stick to the glue outline.
6. Using diluted glue/water solution, child gently paints inside the dinosaur, being careful to cover it all without touching the outline.
7. Child returns to the box and sprinkles a different color "sand" on the painted area.
8. Eyes and other details can be added with more glue and dark sand.
9. Put name on edge of paper and set aside to dry.
10. When dry the teacher can cut around the dinosaur and place it on the bulletin board in a palm, fern, lake, volcano setting if desired.

FINGER PRINTED STEGOSAURUS

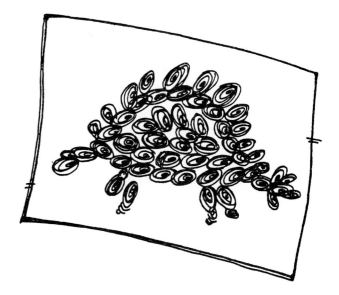

APPROXIMATE TIME: 15 minutes

OBJECTIVES - Students will:
1. create a Stegosaurus print.
2. review and/or discuss the attributes of Stegosaurus.
3. experiment with a new art medium, using an ink pad to make a print. (You could also use tempera)
4. use size and spatial concepts such as low, medium, high and vertical.
5. identify the index finger, thumb and small finger.

MATERIALS PER 8 STUDENTS:
1. Eight 5" x 8" index cards
2. Four stamp pads (preferably black ink)
3. Cloths or wet paper towels for wiping hands
4. Pencils for writing names
5. Aprons

SUGGESTED LITERATURE:
   Patrick's Dinosaurs, Carol Carrick

LANGUAGE/THINKING SKILLS: Let's review and/or discuss some facts about Stegosaurus. What do we know about this dinosaur? (He had bony plates on his back, 4 spikes on his tail, his nose to the ground, short legs, he walked on all four legs, he was a plant eater, and he was about the size of an automobile.) Today we are going to make Stegosaurus on a small card using ink and your fingers and thumb. Watch and I will show you how.

PROCEDURES: MODEL ALL STEPS BEFORE CHILDREN BEGIN.
1. Pass out stamp pads to share and index cards.
2. Press the index finger on the stamp pad.
3. With inked index finger, make a curved hill or rainbow shape on the middle of the card. This will be the backbone. Make each print touch another. Print a slightly curved line for the under side of the body.

4. Make the stand-up plates on the back by pressing the index finger on to the ink pad and making vertical prints along the backbone.
5. Continue the same procedure to fill in the body and put the legs on.

6. Use the little finger to put 4 spikes on the tail.
7. Use the thumb or index finger to make some plants, reinforcing the fact the Stegosaurus was a plant eater.
8. Put names on the back.
9. Clean center, wash hands with soap, then remove aprons.

CHALK SHADOW

APPROXIMATE TIME: 25 minutes

OBJECTIVES - Students will:
1. create a chalk shadow dinosaur using templates and colored chalk.
2. learn a new art technique.
3. be exposed to new vocabulary such as positive, negative, overlap, template, and smear.
4. apply listening skills by following specific directions.

MATERIALS PER 8 STUDENTS:
1. Vibrant colors of chalk
2. Eight 12" X 18" pieces of white art paper
3. At least 4 tagboard templates, cut out, of dinosaurs approximately 8" in height or width. Use both the positive and negative. (see pattern illustration)
4. Facial tissues (Kleenex type)
5. Wipe cloths for hands

SUGGESTED LITERATURE:
   The Tyrannosaurus Game, Steven Kroll

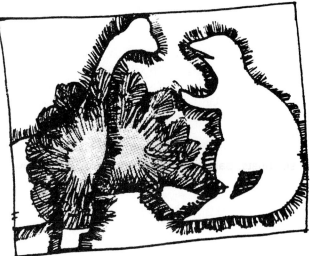

LANGUAGE/THINKING SKILLS: Can you name some of your favorite dinosaurs? (accept all responses) Today we are going to make shadow pictures of some of the dinosaurs. What is a shadow? (A shaded area made when bright light is cast upon a body.) Have you ever made shadow pictures on the wall with your hands and fingers? Today we will use colored chalk and a template or pattern to make dinosaur shadows. If the template is the shape of the dinosaur, we call it a positive template. If the dinosaur shape is cut out, it is called a negative template or pattern. Sometimes when we make the pictures, we can overlap the two templates to create an interesting shadow.

PROCEDURES: BE SURE TO MODEL EACH STEP CAREFULLY.
1. Let each child choose either a positive or negative template, and a piece of colored chalk.
2. Using the chalk, color darkly around the edge of the dinosaur shape. The chalk should extend about 1/2" from the edge.
3. Pass out the white art paper and a tissue.
4. Place the chalked template on the art paper, holding firmly in place with one hand.
5. Using the tissue, gently brush the chalk onto the art paper using straight strokes. This will form a shadow around the positive template, and fill in the center of the negative template.
6. Repeat the procedure for at least two more dinosaurs, overlapping the shadows.
7. Have wipe clothes available for hands.
8. Have children put their names on the back of their papers and set aside for a bulletin board display or room decoration.
9. If desired, mount on colored paper.
10. Have children help clean the area.

DINOSAUR SKELETONS

APPROXIMATE TIME: 25 minutes

OBJECTIVES - Students will:
1. create and construct a skeleton of a dinosaur out of foam packaging material.
2. pretend they are scientists putting dinosaur bones together to determine the skeletal structure.
3. develop fine motor coordination as they work with small objects.
4. listen to vocabulary such as skeleton, skull, scientists, paleontologists, and geologists used in sentences.

MATERIALS PER 8 STUDENTS:
1. Several containers of foam packaging peanuts and stars
2. Eight 12" X 18" sheets of black construction paper
3. White glue
4. Pictures of dinosaur skeletons

SUGGESTED LITERATURE:
Big Old Bones, Carol Carrick

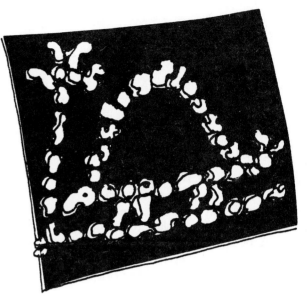

LANGUAGE/THINKING SKILLS: How do scientists know that dinosaurs really lived? (They discovered the bones.) Do you remember what they call bones that are all hooked together to make a shape? (a skeleton) A scientist who looks for old bones is called a paleontologist. Sometimes a scientist called a geologist helps dig in the rocks to find fossils. Other scientists called archaeologists also look for bones by digging in ground. Perhaps someday some of you will be scientists. Today we are all going to pretend we are scientists who have discovered some bones which must be put together to make the skeleton of a dinosaur. Let's look at some pictures of skeletons, and see if we can create some of our own.

PROCEDURES: COVER TABLES WITH PAPER BEFORE STARTING PROJECT
1. Pass out construction paper and place foam peanuts and stars in front of the children.
2. Adult squirts a line of white glue on the paper-covered table above each child's construction paper.
3. Children take the foam pieces, dip them into glue, and arrange them on their paper to form a skeleton of any dinosaur.
4. They may also form trees and plants, if they like.
5. Put names on papers with a pencil.
6. Have children help clean up the area.
7. If time permits, read the suggested literature or another favorite dinosaur book.

SWIMMING ELASMOSAURUS

APPROXIMATE TIME: 30 minutes total, 20 for first session, 10 for second session

OBJECTIVES - Students will:
1. make a "lake" using a tissue paper and diluted white glue technique.
2. discuss Elasmosaurus and the fact that it was a swimmer.
3. practice cutting on curved lines by cutting dittoed Elasmosaurus.
4. make Elasmosaurus "swim" in the "lake."

MATERIALS PER STUDENT:
1. One 9" X 12" tagboard
2. One 12" X 18" light blue tissue paper
3. One 9" X 12" dark blue tissue paper
4. Diluted white glue (1-1) in containers to share
5. Paint brush and scissors
6. One 6" X 9" ditto with Elasmosaurus (see illustration)
7. White glue

SUGGESTED LITERATURE:
What Happened to Patrick's Dinosaurs, Carol Carrick

LANGUAGE/THINKING SKILLS: Elasmosaurus was a swimming dinosaur. He had a very long, thin neck and a big body. What would Elasmosaurus eat? (fish) He had four fins that were so large that they looked like paddles. What were these used for? (to propel him through the water and control the direction that he swam) We are going to make a "lake" using tissue paper and watered down glue. On another day, when lake is dry, we will cut out an Elasmosaurus and make it "swim" in the "lake."

PROCEDURES FOR MAKING THE LAKE:
1. Pass out one piece of tagboard, one piece of light blue tissue paper and one piece of dark blue tissue to each child.
2. Children may cut or tear several thicknesses of tissue into 2"-3" pieces.
3. Next, paint tagboard with diluted glue, a small area at a time, and place single pieces of torn or cut tissue on the painted tagboard stretching paper flat while overlapping each piece. They should cover all the tagboard.
4. After all tissue is in place, gently paint the entire "lake" with more diluted glue. Set aside to dry. Make sure names are on the back.
5. When dry, adult will cut a long slit in the "lake."

PROCEDURES FOR MAKING ELASMOSAURUS :
1. Pass out dittoed Elasmosaurus. Children cut on curved lines.
2. Pass out one popsicle stick to each child. Adult puts a small line of glue on end of the stick.
3. Place Elasmosaurus on glue, and hold until it sticks.
4. Gently slide the stick into the slit in the "lake."
5. Carefully move the stick from side to side so that Elasmosaurus looks as though he is swimming through the water. Have children help clean the center.

PEANUT BUTTER DINOSAURS - COOKING

APPROXIMATE TIME: 25 minutes

OBJECTIVES - Students will:
1. create a dinosaur with edible clay-like dough.
2. participate in a cooperative effort.
3. practice following a recipe.
4. eat a nourishing snack.

MATERIALS PER 8 STUDENTS:
1. 1/2 cup measuring cup
2. Tablespoon
3. Spoon for stirring
4. Bowls and spoons for ingredients
5. Eight paper plates
6. Ingredients for dough (see recipe)
7. Small plastic models of dinosaurs

RECIPE FOR 8:
1/2 cup wheat germ
1/2 cup powdered milk
1/2 cup peanut butter
1/2 cup honey
8 Tablespoons oatmeal

SUGGESTED LITERATURE:
My Visit To The Dinosaurs, Aliki

LANGUAGE/THINKING SKILLS: I'll bet that when you came to school today you didn't know that you would be eating a dinosaur! Today we are going to make a healthy, good-to-eat dough. Then we will use it like clay and form any dinosaur you wish. (Ask what kinds they might make and remind them of some of the features they might want to include on their model.) After you form your dinosaurs, you will pretend that you are a meat eating dinosaur and you will devour your dough dinosaur!

PROCEDURES:
1. Cover the tables with white butcher paper.
2. Have children wash their hands with soap.
3. Arrange the ingredients in the center of the table and let children take turns adding all ingredients into large bowl (except oatmeal) and stirring.
4. Each child will measure 1 Tablespoon of oatmeal onto a paper plate in front of him/her.
5. Adult divides dough into 8 portions and places a portion on each child's plate.
6. Children roll the dough in the oatmeal and form it into their favorite dinosaur. If still too sticky, add more oatmeal.
7. Eat and enjoy. While children are eating their dinosaurs, you may wish to read an Aliki book about dinosaurs.
8. Have children help clean the center and wash their hands.

DIMETRODON DEVILED EGGS

APPROXIMATE TIME: 25 minutes

OBJECTIVES - Students will:
1. prepare a nutritious snack that looks like a dimetrodon
2. follow a recipe.
3. discuss the way dinosaurs prepared nests to lay their eggs.
4. go on a dinosaur egg hunt.
5. use their imaginations.

MATERIALS PER GROUP OF 8 STUDENTS:
1. Eight hard boiled eggs
2. Mayonnaise in a bowl (1/2 cup)
3. Mustard in a bowl (1/4 cup)
4. Salt and pepper in shakers
5. Eight whole pitted black olives
6. Eight pickle chips
7. Two 1 tsp. measuring spoons
8. Eight plastic knives and forks
9. Eight paper plates
10. Eight paper bowls

SUGGESTED LITERATURE:
  Chickens Aren't The Only Ones, Ruth Heller

LANGUAGE/THINKING SKILLS: IF A DINOSAUR EGG HUNT IS GOING TO TAKE PLACE, ADULT MUST HIDE EGGS ON THE PLAYGROUND BEFORE CHILDREN COME TO THE CENTER. A LARGE BOWL OR BASKET WILL BE NEEDED TO COLLECT EGGS.
Can anyone think of an animal that lays eggs? (bird, hen, tortoise, frog, dinosaur, etc.) Dinosaurs laid eggs also. Does anyone know what a dinosaur nest might have looked like? (a large hole in the mud about 3 ft. deep and 6 ft. wide, cover with mud and twigs) Today we are going to go onto the playground and look for dinosaur eggs. Everyone may collect one egg.

PROCEDURES: COLLECT EGGS FROM NESTS ON THE PLAYGROUND.
1. Children wash hands and "dinosaur egg."
2. Pass out paper plates.
3. Crack eggs. Peel onto paper plates and wash again if necessary.
4. Help children cut eggs in half. (if help is needed)
5. Pass out 1 paper bowl to each child. Children will scoop egg yolk into individual bowls and mash with fork.
6. Place mayonnaise and mustard bowls in center of table. Each child will measure one tsp. mayonnaise into his/her bowl and a dash of mustard, salt, and pepper.
7. Mix thoroughly and stuff egg white.
8. Cut pickle chips in half for each child to place in egg yolk to make the backbones of the two dinosaurs.
9. Give each child an olive to cut in half for the dinosaur heads.
10. Eat and enjoy!
11. Have children help clean center.

DINOSAUR DELICACIES - COOKING

APPROXIMATE TIME: 25 minutes

OBJECTIVES - Students will:
1. prepare and sample foods from the meat and vegetable groups to reinforce the concept that some dinosaurs were carnivores and some were herbivores.
2. listen and respond to specific questions about the diets of dinosaurs as previously learned.
3. enjoy a healthy snack
4. discuss the various dinosaurs.

MATERIALS PER STUDENT:
1. Alfalfa sprouts
2. Two celery sticks
3. Four or five goldfish crackers
4. Tuna mixed with mayonnaise
5. Slice of bologna or pieces of bologna (If dinosaur cookie cutters are used, each child will need one slice of bologna, if not, allow 1/4 slice per child.)
6. Dinosaur cookie cutters (optional)
7. Paper plates and forks
8. Spoon for tuna

SUGGESTED LITERATURE:
Danny And The Dinosaur, Syd Hoff

LANGUAGE/THINKING SKILLS: Some dinosaurs ate only plants, and they were called herbivores. Other dinosaurs were meat eaters and they were called carnivores. Where did plant eaters find their food? (on bushes and trees, in swamp areas, etc.) Where did meat eaters find their food? (They ate other dinosaurs.) What were the meat eaters teeth like? (very sharp and large) What were the teeth of plant eaters like? (small in size, not too sharp, often used to grind the food) Today you are going to pretend that you are different kinds of dinosaurs and you will choose what type of food you will eat.

PROCEDURES: PLACE FOOD IN THE MIDDLE OF TABLE.
1. After washing hands, have children take a paper plate and move around the table, taking a pinch of sprouts, two celery sticks, 4-5 goldfish crackers, a slice of bologna, and a heaping spoon of tuna.
2. Give each child a dinosaur cookie cutter and let him cut out his dinosaur and place it on the plate with the rest.
3. Discuss the following question about each dinosaur.
   If you were a _____ which food would you eat and why?
   Brontosaurus: Sprouts because it had very tiny teeth and was not able to chew well, so it ate the marshy grass along the lakes.
   Stegosaurus: Celery Stalks - They were able to eat plants that were a little tougher than the Brontosaurus; they ate bushes.
   Tyrannosaurus Rex: Bologna, because it was a meat eater and ate other dinosaurs.
   Elasmosaurus: Either tuna or fish crackers because it swam and ate fish.
   Pteronadon: Tuna or fish crackers because it flew and swooped down to scoop fish from water.
4. Let children eat food and if time, trace dinosaur shapes on plate.

LITERATURE LIST

Little Blue and Little Yellow, Leo Lionni 16

Mouse Paint, Ellen Stoll Walsh 17

I Love Colors, Stan and Jan Berenstain 18

Planting A Rainbow, Lois Ehlert 19

Shapes, John J. Reiss 21

Color Zoo, Lois Ehlert 22

Freight Train, Donald Crews 23

The Little Engine That Could, Watty Piper 24

Curious George Visits a Police Station, Margaret Rey and Alan J. Shalleek 26

I Read Signs, Tana Hoban 27

Red Light, Green Light, Margaret Wise Brown 28

Dinosaurs, Beware!, Marc Brown and Stephen Krensky 29

Smokey The Bear, Jane Werner Watson 30

Fire Engines, Anne Rockwell 31

Poinsettia And The Firefighters, Felicia Bond 32

Fire! Fire!, Gail Gibbons 33

In 1492, Jean Marzollo 36

Six Crows, Leo Lionni 40

Pumpkin, Pumpkin, Jeanne Titherington 42

The Little Old Lady Who Was Not Afraid of Anything, Linda Williams 43

The Biggest Pumpkin Ever, Steven Kroll 44

Mousekins's Golden House, Edna Miller 45

Little Monster, Joanne and David Wylie 46

Scary, Scary Halloween, Eve Bunting 47

Gus Was a Friendly Ghost, Jane Thayer 48

A Book of Ghosts, Pam Adams and Carl Jones 49

Rotten Ralph's Trick or Treat, Jack Gantos 50

Indian Two Feet and His Horse, Margaret Friskey 54

Boat Ride with Lillian Two Blossom, Patricia Polacco 55

Totem Pole, Diane Hoyt-Goldsmith 56

Arrow to the Sun, Gerald Mc Dermott 57

Knots on a Counting Rope, Bill Martin Jr. 58

The Legend of the Indian Paintbrush, Tommie de Paola 59

Thanksgiving Day, Gail Gibbons 60

Sarah Morton's Day, Kate Waters 61

Oh, What a Thanksgiving!, Steven Kroll 62

Sometimes It's Turkey - Sometimes It's Feathers, Lorna Balian 65

Mousekin's Thanksgiving, Edna Miller 66

It's Thanksgiving, Jack Prelutsky 67

Corn Is Maize, Aliki 68

From Grass to Butter, Ali Mitgutsch 69

Rain Makes Applesauce, Julian Scheer 70

Stone Soup, Marcia Brown 71

Santa's Hat, Claire Schumacher 74

My Christmas Stocking, Matthew Price 75

The Night Before Christmas, Clement Moore 76

Imogene's Antlers, David Small 77

Rudolph The Red Nosed Reindeer, Robert L. May 77

Wake Up, Bear, It's Christmas, Stephen Gammel 78

Max's Christmas, Rosemary Wells 79

Night Tree, Eve Bunting 80

The Little Fir Tree, Margaret Wise Brown 81

The Night Before Christmas, Clement Moore 82

The Polar Express, Chris Van Allsburg 83

The Twelve Days of Christmas, Jan Brett 84

Hansel and Gretel, Paul O. Zelinsky 85

My First Hanukkah Book, Aileen Fisher 88

Potato Pancakes All Around, Marilyn Hirsh 89

First Snow, Emily McCully 91

Snow is Falling, Franklyn M. Branley 92

The Mitten, Alvin Tresselt 93

Snowy Day, Ezra Jack Keats 94

Midnight Snowman, Caroline Feller Bauer 95

On Mothers Lap, Ann Herbert Scott 96

Very Last First Time, Jan Andrews 97

Alaska ABC Book, Charlene Kreeger and Shannon Cartwright 98

Tacky the Penguin, Helen Lester 99

A Picture Book of Martin Luther King, Jr., David Adler 102

Dinosaurs Are Different, Aliki 104

Patrick's Dinosaurs, Carol Carrick 105

The Tyrannosaurus Game, Steven Kroll 106

Big Old Bones, Carol Carrick 107

What Happened to Patrick's Dinosaurs, Carol Carrick 108

My Visit To The Dinosaurs, Aliki 109

Chickens Aren't The Only Ones, Ruth Heller 110

Danny And The Dinosaur, Syd Hoff 111

USING CALENDAR CAPERS

CALENDAR CAPERS make calendar time a daily math lesson! Children discover patterns, identify numerals, identify shapes, practice counting and counting on, predict numerals and shapes, practice sequencing, and develop vocabulary.

The school year calendar begins with a simple, two-shape pattern. Each month a new patterning challenge is added to extend the thinking skills of the students. All calendar pieces have been designed to coordinate with the themes in **KINDER CAPERS**.

The calendar pieces are designed to fit in hanging calendar charts with 3 1/2-inch plastic pockets. For added durability mount calendar dates on poster board and laminate them before cutting them apart.

SEPTEMBER

BEGINNING SHAPES
CIRCLE/SQUARE PATTERN

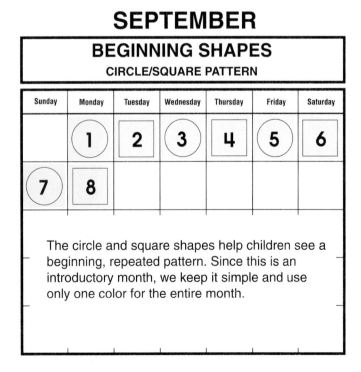

The circle and square shapes help children see a beginning, repeated pattern. Since this is an introductory month, we keep it simple and use only one color for the entire month.

OCTOBER

ADVANCED SHAPES
TRIANGLE/RECTANGLE/OVAL/DIAMOND PATTERN

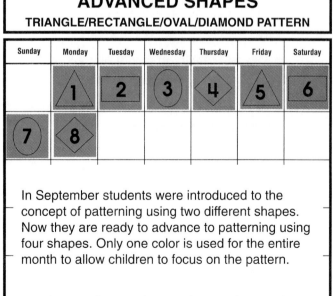

In September students were introduced to the concept of patterning using two different shapes. Now they are ready to advance to patterning using four shapes. Only one color is used for the entire month to allow children to focus on the pattern.

©The Education Center, Inc. • *Kinder Capers—Fall*

NOVEMBER

FALL LEAVES
GOLD/ORANGE/TAN PATTERN

Sunday	Monday	Tuesday	Wednesday	Thursday	Friday	Saturday
	1	2	3	4	5	6
7	8					

The November calendar introduces students to the fall season and to the concept of using different colors to create a pattern. Since the concept of a three-color pattern is new, it is important to use only one leaf shape.

DECEMBER

ORNAMENTS
RED/GREEN/GOLD/BLUE PATTERN

Sunday	Monday	Tuesday	Wednesday	Thursday	Friday	Saturday
	1	2	3	4	5	6
7	8					

Now that students have had the experience of using three colors to create a pattern, they are ready to advance to a four-color pattern. Again it is important to keep the ornament shape the same. By introducing one concept at a time, students will be successful!

JANUARY

MITTENS
LEFT/RIGHT PATTERN

Sunday	Monday	Tuesday	Wednesday	Thursday	Friday	Saturday
	1	2	3	4	5	6
7	8					

January mittens offer the perfect opportunity to introduce and/or practice the concept of left and right. Have the students put their left or right hands in the air and chant the pattern, while you point to the mittens on the calendar. After going through the month practicing left and right, many students will have internalized the concept.

ANY TIME

DINOSAURS
TYRANN. REX/TRICERATOPS/STEGOSAURUS/APATOSAURUS

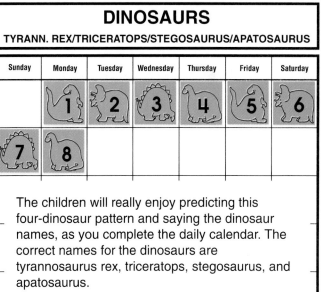

Sunday	Monday	Tuesday	Wednesday	Thursday	Friday	Saturday
	1	2	3	4	5	6
7	8					

The children will really enjoy predicting this four-dinosaur pattern and saying the dinosaur names, as you complete the daily calendar. The correct names for the dinosaurs are tyrannosaurus rex, triceratops, stegosaurus, and apatosaurus.

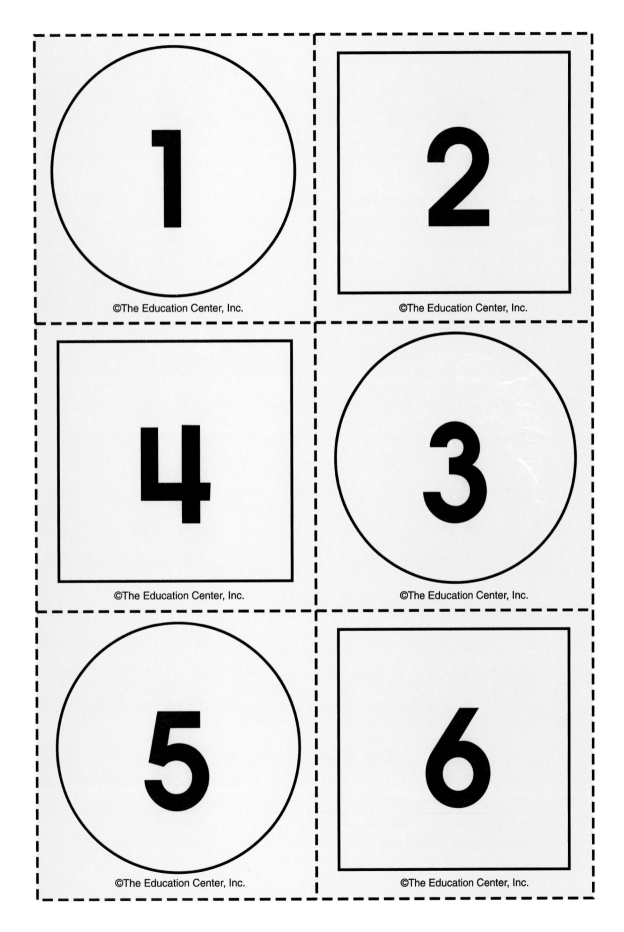

1
©The Education Center, Inc.

2
©The Education Center, Inc.

4
©The Education Center, Inc.

3
©The Education Center, Inc.

5
©The Education Center, Inc.

6
©The Education Center, Inc.

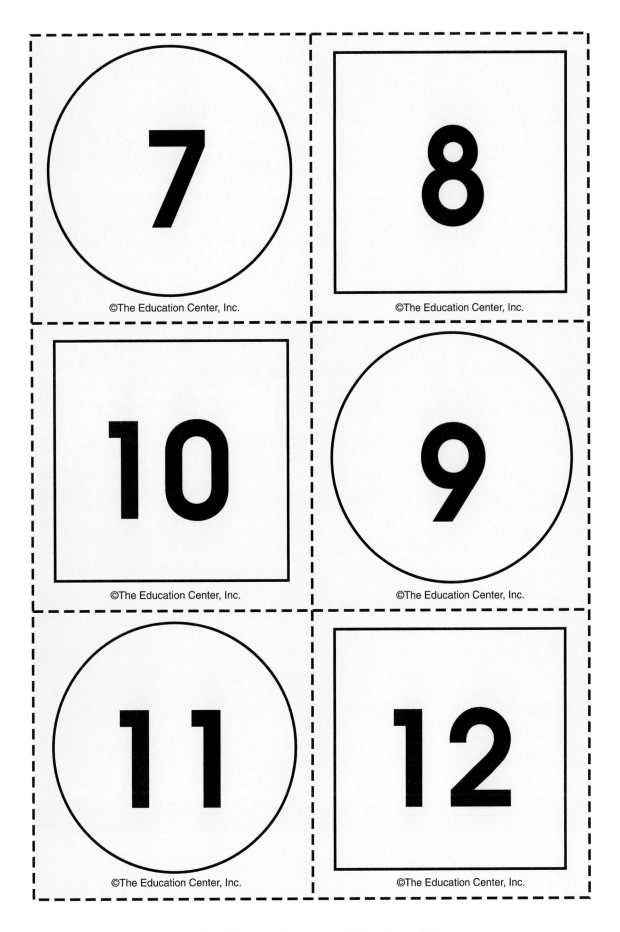

7 ©The Education Center, Inc.

8 ©The Education Center, Inc.

10 ©The Education Center, Inc.

9 ©The Education Center, Inc.

11 ©The Education Center, Inc.

12 ©The Education Center, Inc.

13
©The Education Center, Inc.

14
©The Education Center, Inc.

16
©The Education Center, Inc.

15
©The Education Center, Inc.

17
©The Education Center, Inc.

18
©The Education Center, Inc.

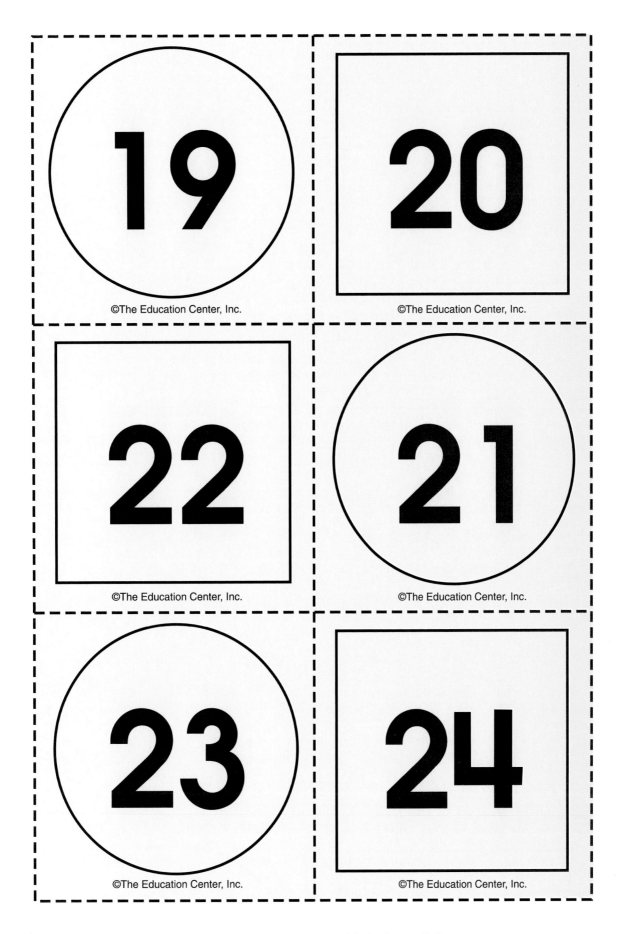

19

©The Education Center, Inc.

20

©The Education Center, Inc.

22

©The Education Center, Inc.

21

©The Education Center, Inc.

23

©The Education Center, Inc.

24

©The Education Center, Inc.

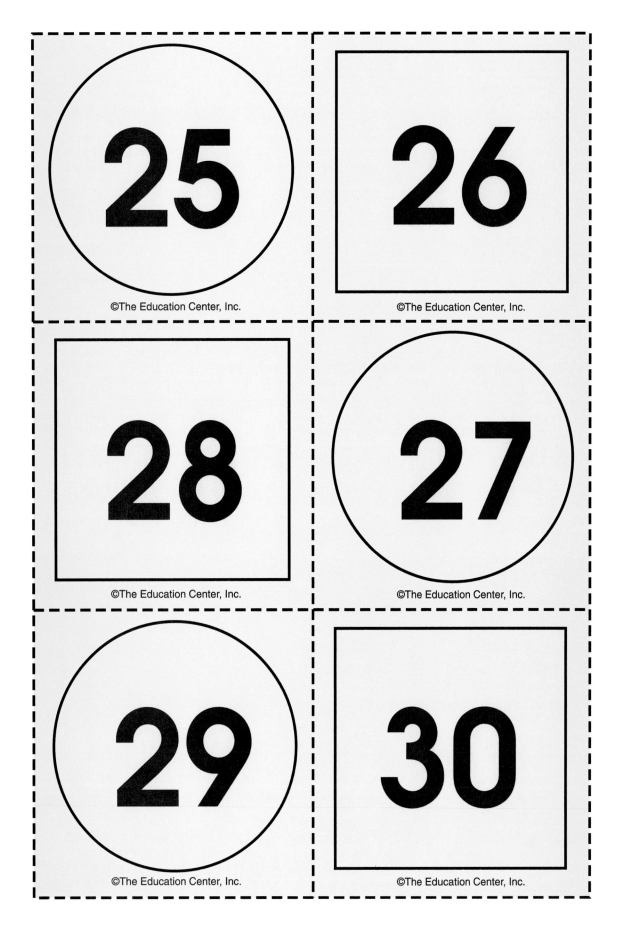

25 ©The Education Center, Inc.

26 ©The Education Center, Inc.

28 ©The Education Center, Inc.

27 ©The Education Center, Inc.

29 ©The Education Center, Inc.

30 ©The Education Center, Inc.

31

©The Education Center, Inc.

©The Education Center, Inc.

©The Education Center, Inc.

©The Education Center, Inc.

©The Education Center, Inc.

©The Education Center, Inc.

1
©The Education Center, Inc.

2
©The Education Center, Inc.

3
©The Education Center, Inc.

4
©The Education Center, Inc.

5
©The Education Center, Inc.

6
©The Education Center, Inc.

7
©The Education Center, Inc.

8
©The Education Center, Inc.

9
©The Education Center, Inc.

10
©The Education Center, Inc.

11
©The Education Center, Inc.

12
©The Education Center, Inc.

13 ©The Education Center, Inc.

14 ©The Education Center, Inc.

15 ©The Education Center, Inc.

16 ©The Education Center, Inc.

17 ©The Education Center, Inc.

18 ©The Education Center, Inc.

19

©The Education Center, Inc.

20

©The Education Center, Inc.

21

©The Education Center, Inc.

22

©The Education Center, Inc.

23

©The Education Center, Inc.

24

©The Education Center, Inc.

25 ©The Education Center, Inc.

26 ©The Education Center, Inc.

27 ©The Education Center, Inc.

28 ©The Education Center, Inc.

29 ©The Education Center, Inc.

30 ©The Education Center, Inc.

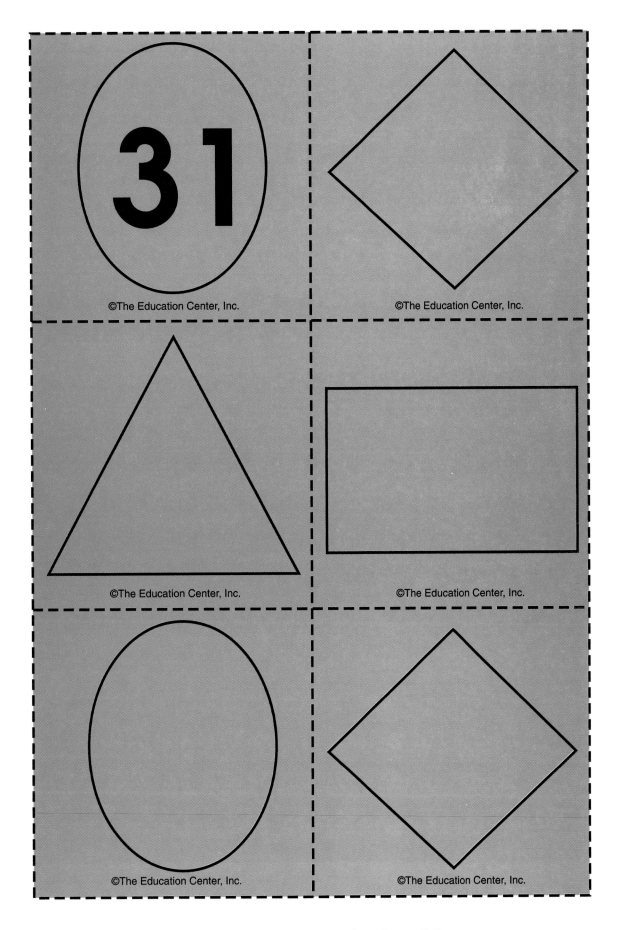

31

©The Education Center, Inc.

©The Education Center, Inc.

©The Education Center, Inc.

©The Education Center, Inc.

©The Education Center, Inc.

©The Education Center, Inc.

1

4

7

10

13

©The Education Center, Inc.

©The Education Center, Inc.

©The Education Center, Inc.

©The Education Center, Inc.

©The Education Center, Inc.

©The Education Center, Inc.

2
©The Education Center, Inc.

5
©The Education Center, Inc.

8
©The Education Center, Inc.

11
©The Education Center, Inc.

14
©The Education Center, Inc.

©The Education Center, Inc.

3 ©The Education Center, Inc.

6 ©The Education Center, Inc.

9 ©The Education Center, Inc.

12 ©The Education Center, Inc.

15 ©The Education Center, Inc.

©The Education Center, Inc.

16 ©The Education Center, Inc.

19 ©The Education Center, Inc.

22 ©The Education Center, Inc.

25 ©The Education Center, Inc.

28 ©The Education Center, Inc.

31 ©The Education Center, Inc.

17
©The Education Center, Inc.

20
©The Education Center, Inc.

23
©The Education Center, Inc.

26
©The Education Center, Inc.

29
©The Education Center, Inc.

©The Education Center, Inc.

18
©The Education Center, Inc.

21
©The Education Center, Inc.

24
©The Education Center, Inc.

27
©The Education Center, Inc.

30
©The Education Center, Inc.

©The Education Center, Inc.

1

5

9

13

©The Education Center, Inc.

©The Education Center, Inc.

©The Education Center, Inc.

©The Education Center, Inc.

©The Education Center, Inc.

©The Education Center, Inc.

2 ©The Education Center, Inc.

6 ©The Education Center, Inc.

10 ©The Education Center, Inc.

14 ©The Education Center, Inc.

©The Education Center, Inc.

©The Education Center, Inc.

3 ©The Education Center, Inc.

7 ©The Education Center, Inc.

11 ©The Education Center, Inc.

15 ©The Education Center, Inc.

©The Education Center, Inc.

©The Education Center, Inc.

4 ©The Education Center, Inc.

8 ©The Education Center, Inc.

12 ©The Education Center, Inc.

16 ©The Education Center, Inc.

©The Education Center, Inc.

©The Education Center, Inc.

17
©The Education Center, Inc.

21
©The Education Center, Inc.

25
©The Education Center, Inc.

29
©The Education Center, Inc.

©The Education Center, Inc.

©The Education Center, Inc.

18
©The Education Center, Inc.

22
©The Education Center, Inc.

26
©The Education Center, Inc.

30
©The Education Center, Inc.

©The Education Center, Inc.

©The Education Center, Inc.

19 ©The Education Center, Inc.

23 ©The Education Center, Inc.

27 ©The Education Center, Inc.

31 ©The Education Center, Inc.

©The Education Center, Inc.

©The Education Center, Inc.

20 ©The Education Center, Inc.

24 ©The Education Center, Inc.

28 ©The Education Center, Inc.

©The Education Center, Inc.

©The Education Center, Inc.

©The Education Center, Inc.

©The Education Center, Inc.

©The Education Center, Inc.

©The Education Center, Inc.

©The Education Center, Inc.

©The Education Center, Inc.

©The Education Center, Inc.

©The Education Center, Inc.

©The Education Center, Inc.

©The Education Center, Inc.

©The Education Center, Inc.

©The Education Center, Inc.

©The Education Center, Inc.

13 ©The Education Center, Inc.

14 ©The Education Center, Inc.

15 ©The Education Center, Inc.

16 ©The Education Center, Inc.

17 ©The Education Center, Inc.

18 ©The Education Center, Inc.

19
©The Education Center, Inc.

20
©The Education Center, Inc.

21
©The Education Center, Inc.

22
©The Education Center, Inc.

23
©The Education Center, Inc.

24
©The Education Center, Inc.

25
©The Education Center, Inc.

26
©The Education Center, Inc.

27
©The Education Center, Inc.

28
©The Education Center, Inc.

29
©The Education Center, Inc.

30
©The Education Center, Inc.

©The Education Center, Inc.

©The Education Center, Inc.

©The Education Center, Inc.

©The Education Center, Inc.

©The Education Center, Inc.

©The Education Center, Inc.

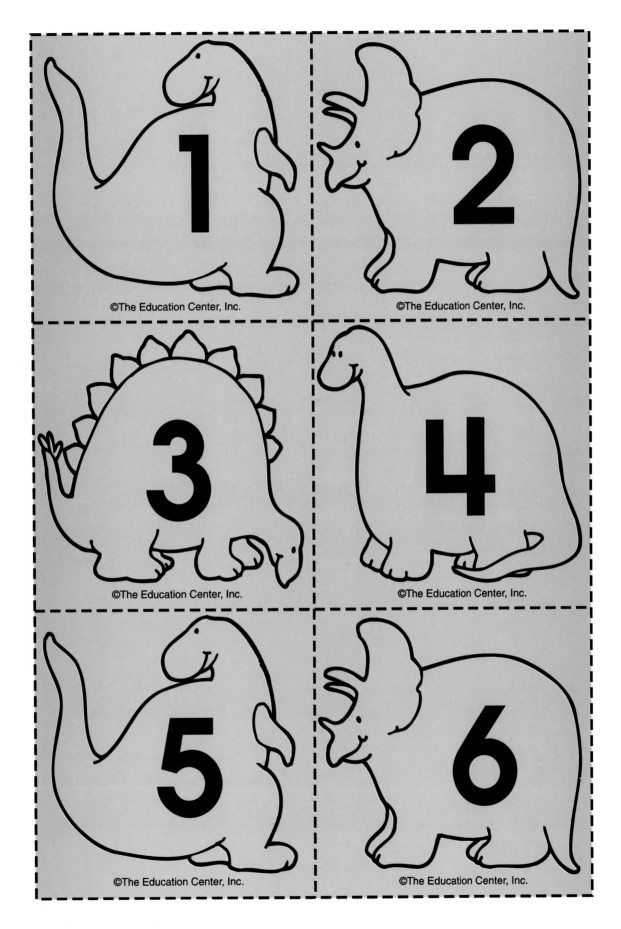

©The Education Center, Inc.

©The Education Center, Inc.

©The Education Center, Inc.

©The Education Center, Inc.

©The Education Center, Inc.

©The Education Center, Inc.

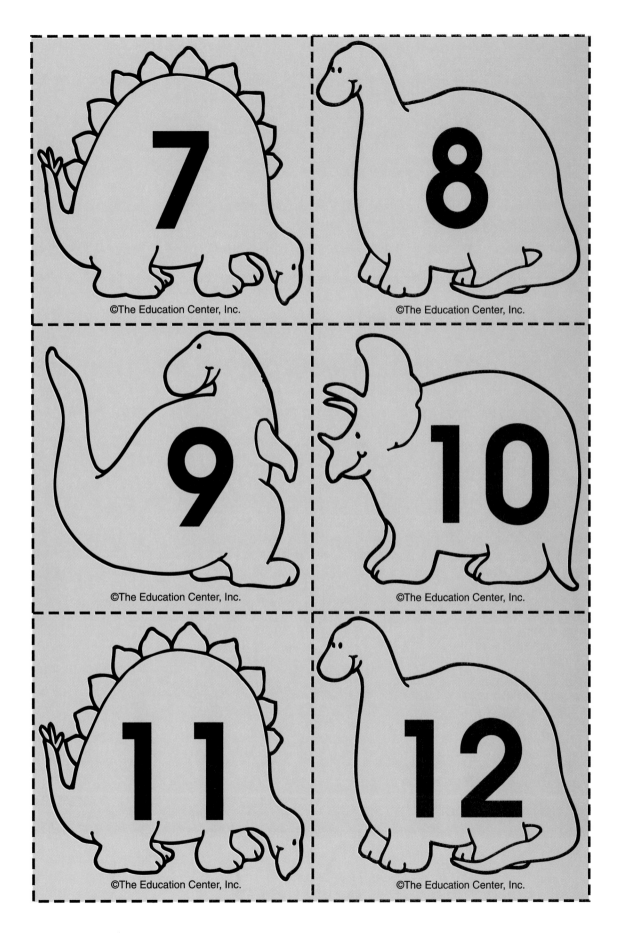

7 ©The Education Center, Inc.

8 ©The Education Center, Inc.

9 ©The Education Center, Inc.

10 ©The Education Center, Inc.

11 ©The Education Center, Inc.

12 ©The Education Center, Inc.

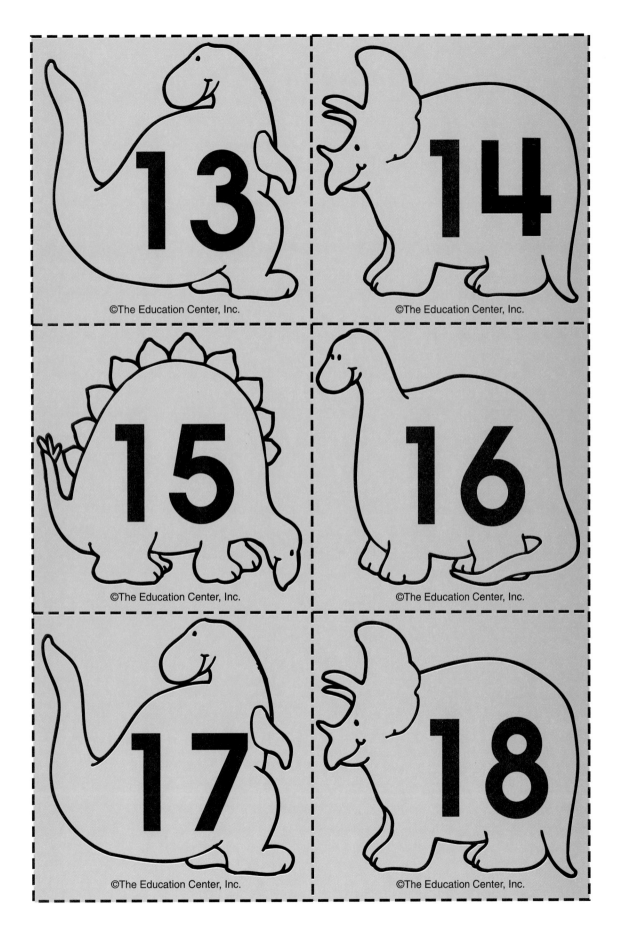

©The Education Center, Inc.

©The Education Center, Inc.

©The Education Center, Inc.

©The Education Center, Inc.

©The Education Center, Inc.

©The Education Center, Inc.

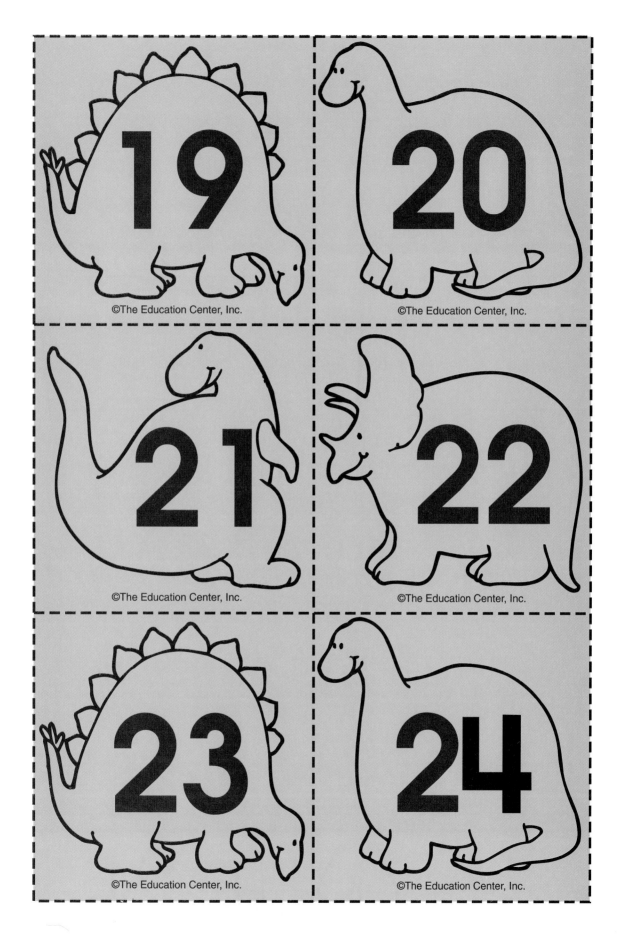

©The Education Center, Inc.

©The Education Center, Inc.

©The Education Center, Inc.

©The Education Center, Inc.

©The Education Center, Inc.

©The Education Center, Inc.

25 ©The Education Center, Inc.

26 ©The Education Center, Inc.

27 ©The Education Center, Inc.

28 ©The Education Center, Inc.

29 ©The Education Center, Inc.

30 ©The Education Center, Inc.

©The Education Center, Inc.

©The Education Center, Inc.

©The Education Center, Inc.

©The Education Center, Inc.

©The Education Center, Inc.

©The Education Center, Inc.